Principles of
SUPERVISION

DANTES/DSST* Test Study Guide

All rights reserved. This Study Guide, Book and Flashcards are protected under the US Copyright Law. No part of this book or study guide or flashcards may be reproduced, distributed or stored in a retrieval system, or transmitted in any form or by any means, electronic, mechanical, photocopying, recording, or otherwise, without the prior written permission of the publisher Breely Crush Publishing, LLC.

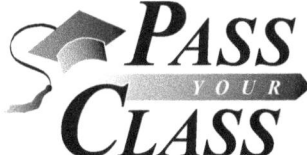

© 2026 Breely Crush Publishing, LLC

*DSST is a registered trademark of The Thomson Corporation and its affiliated companies, and does not endorse this book.

971122625143

Copyright ©2003 - 2026, Breely Crush Publishing, LLC.

All rights reserved.

This Study Guide, Book and Flashcards are protected under the US Copyright Law. No part of this publication may be reproduced, distributed or stored in a retrieval system, or transmitted in any form or by any means, electronic, mechanical, photocopying, recording, or otherwise, without the prior written permission of the publisher Breely Crush Publishing, LLC.

Published by Breely Crush Publishing, LLC
10808 River Front Parkway
South Jordan, UT 84095
www.breelycrushpublishing.com

ISBN-10: 1-61433-687-3
ISBN-13: 978-1-61433-687-7

Printed and bound in the United States of America.

**DSST is a registered trademark of The Thomson Corporation and its affiliated companies, and does not endorse this book.*

Table of Contents

What is a Supervisor? 1
What Does it Take to be a Supervisor? 1
Authority 1
Planning 2
Steps in Planning 3
Mission Statement 3
Goals and Objectives 4
Policies 4
Procedures and Rules 4
Decision Making 5
Change 5
Time Management 6
Delegation 7
Organizing 7
Organizational Theories 8
Organizational Structures 9
Line and Staff Authority 11
Line and Functional Authority 11
Delegation of Authority 11
Unity of Command 12
Centralization and Decentralization 12
Organization Charts 13
Matrix and Project Organizations 14
Staffing 15
Directing 15
Management by Walking Around (MBWA) 16
Job Satisfaction 18
Job Enrichment vs. Job Enlargement 19
Maslow's Hierarchy of Needs 19
Leadership 20
Contingency Leadership 22
Path-Goal Model 23
Vroom-Yetton Model 24
Lifecycle Model 25
Vertical-Dyad Linkages 26
Motivation 27
Hawthorne Effect 28
Theory X & Y 28
Communication 28

Communication/Information Flow in an Organizational Setting	*30*
Group Dynamics	*30*
Problem Solving	*30*
Conflict Resolution	*31*
Recruiting and Selecting Talent	*32*
Working with a Diverse Workforce	*33*
Discipline	*34*
Employee Counseling	*35*
Controlling & Budgets	*35*
Gantt Charts	*36*
Legal Issues	*39*
Sexual Harassment	*45*
Stress in the Workplace	*46*
Personnel Administration	*47*
Performance Appraisals	*48*
Collective Bargaining and Unions	*50*
Training and Development	*51*
Training Need Analysis	*52*
Organizational Development – OD	*53*
Operations Planning and Control	*53*
Indirect Environmental Influences (Macroenvironment)	*55*
Productivity	*60*
Total Quality Management (TQM)	*60*
Six Sigma	*61*
Work Scheduling	*61*
Business Ethics	*62*
Moral Philosophies & Business Ethics	*66*
Gross Domestic Product (GDP)	*78*
NAFTA and GATT	*81*
Sample Test Questions	*85*
Test Taking Strategies	*127*
Legal Note	*128*

Principles of Supervision

What is a Supervisor?

In a broader sense, a supervisor may be defined as working with people and groups of people with the sole intention of achieving organizational goals. On a specific sense, the role of a supervisor is to do just that, supervise employees. This is not as simple as ensuring that employees perform work but includes leadership, motivation, scheduling and meeting company goals and objectives.

What Does it Take to be a Supervisor?

Supervisors need to be trained in the area that they are required to supervise. This helps greatly when training new employees and correcting current employees in their work habits. This also gives them a greater understanding of the process so that they can suggest improvements to their managers and schedule the correct amount of employees, materials, etc., to ensure that they meet productivity goals and any other company objectives.

Authority

In order to achieve company objectives and to sail smoothly on the chosen direction towards that objective, the superiors need authority to enforce compliance of company policies, procedures and rules by subordinates.

Traditional authority is given to those with a specific title or function such as supervisor or Vice President. Having that type of job and title automatically gives authority. However, just because you may have authority, it doesn't mean that people will do what you say.

Charismatic authority is when people admire, respect and follow someone who may or may not be their "official" leader because of their charismatic personality.

Legal or rational authority is when someone's authority is based on a legal right such as law enforcement, homeowner's enforcement & committees, etc.

© 2026 Breely Crush Publishing, LLC   www.PassYourClass.com

Planning

Planning comprises of setting objectives i.e., goals for the organization as well as developing work-maps that identify the ways and means of achieving such objectives. It is the most basic function of managing and all other functions are built, brick by brick, over it. Broadly speaking it revolves around the selection of not only the total organizational objectives, but departmental, even sectional goals, and more importantly spelling out in clear terms the ways through which such objectives, goals are to be accomplished. What? How? When and Who? is decided in advance at the planning stage. What to do, How to do, When to do and Who exactly will do is the primary objective of good planning. It, therefore, precedes all other managerial functions. Since planning and controlling are related most intricately they become inseparable and therefore, a good plan always spells out yardsticks for accomplishing the planned objective. It is obvious control measures are also part and parcel of a well thought out plan.

Steps in Planning

1. Analysis of opportunities: Thorough knowledge of the plus points of your company and the products, market knowledge, knowledge on competition and knowledge as to what exactly the needs and aspirations of the customer are in so far as the products are concerned.
2. Setting of objectives: An unambiguous objective that spells out clearly where the organization is at the moment and why, where it should be heading, what should be the best direction to get there, what specific action should be taken by whom and when, and what measures should be watched to get information on whether the plan is going on the right track and at the right speed.
3. To identify the basis: The plan has to work in what sort of environment – both external and internal. To take note of all factors that form part of the external environment.
4. To identify, analyze, compare and choose the best of available alternatives.
5. To design relevant plans that are supportive in nature such as purchasing capital goods, purchasing materials, sub-assemblies and components, recruit, train and place needed personnel, etc.
6. Quantify for control: reduce your actions into numbers – in other words work out budgets. Example: volume of business both in quantity and dollar terms for the targeted period, inventory, operating expenses, expenditure on capital goods, sales territory budgets, etc.

There are long term plans such as a 10 year or a 5 year plan which reflects the continuity of policy and short term plans like an annual plan that sets targets for the year to be achieved and which, for the sake of control, is further bifurcated into half yearly, quarterly and even monthly plans.

Mission Statement

The mission statement tells employees and others what is the main purpose of the company is. For example, the purpose of a University is primarily teaching and then doing research on studies. Every organization's principal planning document gives its mission statement explaining what the organization stands for and what its activities are going to be. Example: The mission statement of Du Pont is "…better living through chemistry…."

Goals and Objectives

Objectives are identified goals of an organization towards accomplishment of which all organizational activities are directed. It is an action program specifying what should be achieved over a specified time and what resources are to be employed in achieving such objectives. What is an organization going to do in terms of business, i.e., what business it is aiming at and how it is going about it? What is the time frame, what are the resources and where from they are coming, who all are going to be responsible and who all are accountable for achieving objectives?

Policies

A policy can be defined as a predetermined action course that serves as a guide for the identified and accepted objectives and goals. A policy indicates the management strategy towards attainment of the overall objectives and goals and seeks to establish a platform of guiding principles, which makes delegation of work to lower levels easy.

Procedures and Rules

They can be defined as guides to action. In order to handle future activities one needs a plan that shows clearly what methods are to be used. And this plan that establishes such methods is known as procedure. Procedures are available at every level of an organization. It is more widely adhered to in the lower levels. Some organizations have even departmental procedures cogently spelled out for the people of the department to follow. Rules give us distinct action plans without permitting any sort of discretion whatsoever. The action plan may spell out what action or non-action to be taken in clear terms. They are very simple plans.

Programs contain a simple, complicated or complex plan of activities developed primarily for carrying out stated policies. It simplifies the process of decision-making. A program generally consists of objectives, policies, procedures, rules, individual task allocations, what action or inaction to be taken or not taken by whom and when, and what resources are to be employed in order to successfully carry out a specified goal. Programs are also assisted by appropriate budgets in quantity or dollar terms.

🎓 Decision Making

The core of planning is decision making. There are alternatives available. Choosing the best alternative from a plethora of available alternatives and sticking to it is the focus of decision making.

In decision-making you have to identify the Limiting Factor, which can be defined as something, which stands in the way of achieving a goal. The impediment. Identify the limiting factor or factors and solve them in order to arrive at the best possible decision. How to evaluate alternatives? There are Marginal Analysis Models and Cost-effective Analysis Models. The Marginal Analysis deals in analyzing the additional units of revenue one gets from incurring a certain unit of additional costs. The cost-effective analysis deals in cost-benefit analysis, i.e., the ratio of benefits to costs. Your experience, ability to experiment and an analytical bent of mind helps you to arrive at a rational decision under specific given circumstances. Operations Research lends a scientific aura to management decision-making. There are goals, models, variables, limitations – all such factors are built into quantifiable mathematical terms or formulae to decipher and arrive at the best decision possible under a given circumstance. Not all the managers are equipped mathematically to decide among alternative solutions. It is sometimes difficult to quantify a factor. In such cases operations research can do little about it. There is Risk Analysis, which again is a method steeped in mathematical terms – it tells you what probabilities are there to arrive at decisional outcomes. There are Decision Trees, which again are statistical models which tell us which are the possible decision points, chance events which are likely to occur and what probabilities are there for each course of action. Then there is Preference Theory, which tells you a given manager's willingness to take or refrain from taking (unwillingness) risks.

🎓 Change

Change is the essence of life. There are different levels of changes.

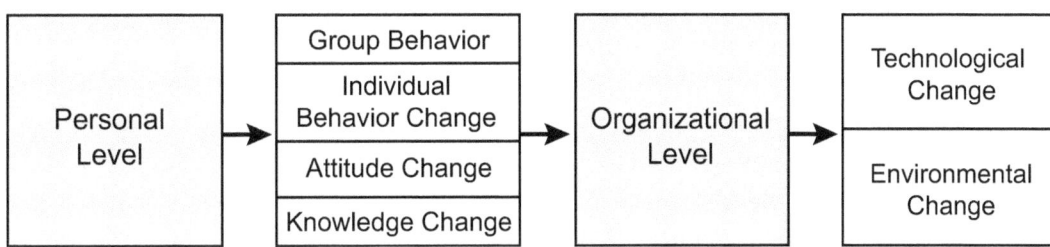

At the personal level knowledge changes are the easiest. Once you read this book you will have gained a little more knowledge than you had before starting it. Attitudinal change is not as difficult as individual behavior change, though time and conscious effort is needed. Group behavior change is a little more difficult than individual behavior change. Group behavior change affects an organization. If people as a group within an organization demand certain things, say, increased rest periods, lesser number of work hours, it impacts the organization and the Personnel Manager has to deal with such a situation. At organizational level, environmental changes – Social, Economic, Political, Legal – any change in any of the components, is going to affect the organization adversely. In the case of technological change, an organization has to face the music, if it does not adapt itself to the changes adeptly and with speed. A change is certainly a limiting factor in the planning process. Rapid changes more especially in the environmental and technological areas impact organizational plans adversely. In the field of computers, the chip capacity of the hard disks increased in breathtaking speed. A 2-Gigabyte hard disk is considered obsolete – as there are 40 and 80 GB hard disks available. Again the increase in speed of chips is breathtaking! Once radios used bulky, noisy, inelegant, vacuum tubes, which became obsolete after Bell laboratories designed transistors! In such rapidly changing, highly competitive environment, it is your own creativity and techniques bordering on innovation that are necessary to exist. Fast adaptability to change is the key.

 ## Time Management

A supervisor has time management responsibilities as well. A supervisor must manage their time and their employee's time collectively to perform. Time management can be simplified to making a series of goals and working backward. For example, a design team must create a brochure for a client. Here are the required steps:

- Create layout
- Create copy
- Choose photographs
- Proofread brochure
- Print brochure
- Present completed project

Based on the required steps to complete this project, a manager can assign an amount of time to each area such as:

- Create layout – 4 hours
- Create copy – 3 hours
- Choose photographs – 2 hours
- Proofread brochure – 1 hour
- Print brochure – 1 day
- Present completed project – 10 minutes

Once you have determined how long each step will take, you can work backwards from the due date to ensure that your work is completed on time. This is also a simplified version of a Gantt chart in a text format.

With other projects, like long term corporate goals, the steps are less tangible. For example, let's say that the corporate goal is to save 10% on manufacturing widgets, which is what your department does. What can you do to reduce costs 10%? You will need to brainstorm your own ideas. A supervisory may think up the following:

- Reduce unnecessary overtime
- Ensure quality of products is at the correct level so that inferior or shoddy products are not completed just to be thrown away
- Review office and other supply orders
- Review discretionary department spending (team rewards and recognition, etc.)

With this type of a project, you will need to create short term and long term goals to reach the goal of saving 10%. You may create a daily goal of creating 100% perfect products. The key to time management is doing the small every day goals and tasks that will build up to be the solution and completion of the long term goal.

Another large part of time management is delegation.

Delegation

Delegation is a way of supervisors to pass on complete or parts of their required tasks onto those that report to them. For example, a line supervisor has a large amount of responsibilities such as training, HR issues, motivating, meeting production goals, corporate meetings, etc. He or she may choose someone on the team to be a "team lead" or a person slightly elevated in responsibility from the others. This person can handle responsibilities delegated to them from the supervisor such as creating the schedule, approving or coordinating days off, creating team building activities or simply being a sounding board for employee concerns.

Organizing

Organizing defines organizational roles to be played by individuals, their positions and the authority relationships. Every role should be clearly defined with distinct objectives in mind. The major duties to be performed by individuals, how responsibilities are to be delegated and with what authority are to be included in the organizing process. It should also indicate what resources are available, what information and tools are necessary to carry out such roles effectively. This is organizing in a nutshell. An <u>informal organization</u> according to Chester Barnard is any joint personal activity without conscious joint purpose, even though possibly contributing to joint results. The relationships in an informal organization never reflect in any organizational chart. There may be sub-assembly groups, stress groups or accounts groups, i.e., groups of individuals. However, each group identifies itself as a contributing member and acts in unison where the group's ideal or any given member's identity or right is challenged.

Organizational Theories

Many theorists propounded a number of theories of which the following 3 are important: (1) Classical Organization Theory, (2) The Mechanistic Theory, and (3) The System Theory. The <u>Classical Organizational Theory</u> deals in specializing job assignments, works towards easy managerial functions, seeks to establish authority structures and delegation of responsibility and authority, maintains bureaucracy which speaks of offices and roles and institutes formal channels of communication among members of different departments in the organization. It deals in division of labor, vertical and horizontal specialization, scalar authority, etc.

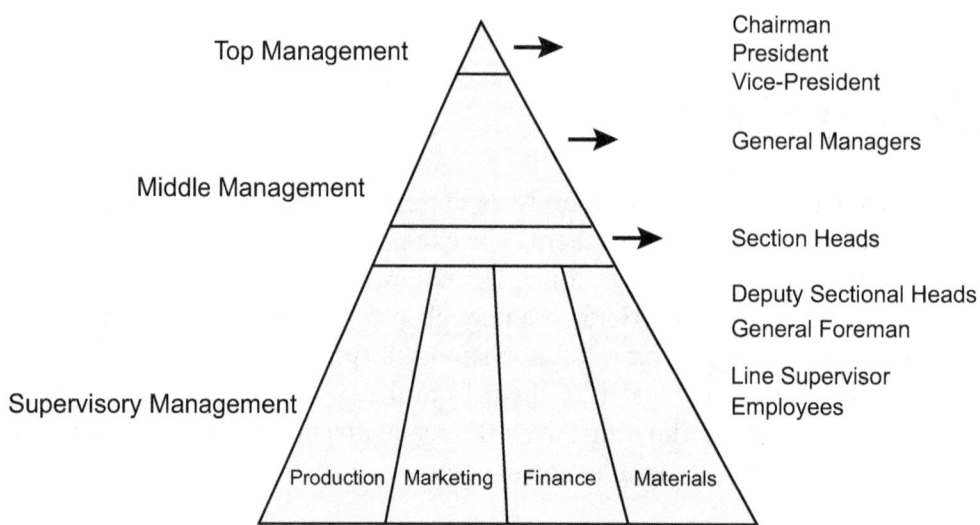

VERTICAL AND HORIZONTAL SPECIALIZATION

<u>The Mechanistic Theory</u> states that organizational change is inevitable and that organizations and people within the organizations have no other choice except following natural law. Industrialization brought in its wake a laissez faire philosophy in political circles, which advocated the integrity or virtue of letting the natural process take its own course. This theory was supported by economic philosophy prevalent at that time.

In a way it is a precursor to the later scientific management movement. The theorists had foreseen the potency of competition. They thought specialization was a tool for obtaining competitive advantage. The later versions of this theory harp on compensation structures. Both the classical organizational and the Mechanistic theories took people for granted. This gradually created uncertainties in the minds of workers and opposition started. This situation necessitated bringing focus on people. Unions and collective bargaining showed their head. Human relations principles were born out of necessity. Approximately 30% of the U.S. workforce is unionized.

The Systems Theory deals with interdependence instead of independence of variables and their interactions. It started with a more intensive, very broad, wide-angle – involving a number of variables to measure complex inter-relationships – and inclusive viewpoint. Group behavior is seen in the system as broadly shaped and influenced. There are various elements in an organizational system but the common choice of an element is the individual in an organization. It identifies the system as changing, evolving and most dynamic. The systems model recognizes the environment of the system and other related variables, which includes all other subsystems and seeks to elucidate an adequate explanation of organizational behavior. The system as a whole is seen as an open system.

Organizational Structures

Any formal organization can be described as an intentional structure of roles. For the sake of functionality, a formal organizational structure is divided into many departments on the basis of their functions. There may be an Accounts department, a Marketing department, a Production department, a Material department, an Engineering department and so on. A department typically has a Head or Boss followed by a Deputy and then the assisting employees. In such a scenario, the roles of the Department Head, the Deputy and the assisting employees should be very clear and the authority relationship should be spelled out. The cooperation of all the people making up a department should be effective in order to achieve the overall organizational objectives. How many people can a department head or his deputy effectively control is the crux of the "Span" of management. There are two types – (1) Narrow Span and (2) Wide Span.

Structure
An Organization with a Narrow Span

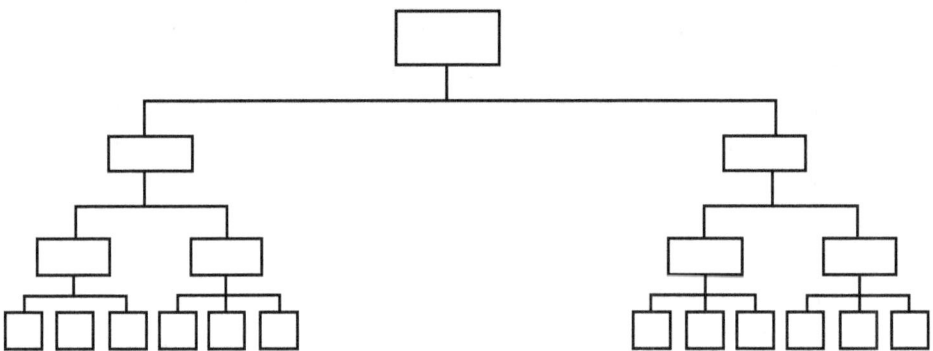

Structure
An Organization with a Wide Span

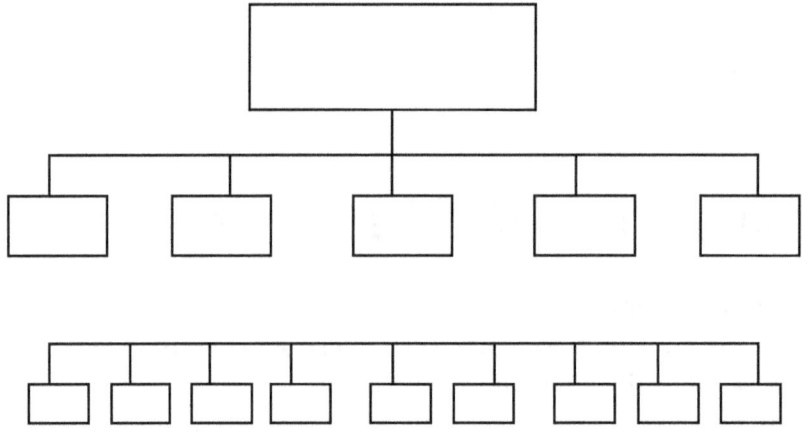

In a narrow span organizational structure, close supervision is possible, good control, and communication between Department Head and subordinates occur quickly. The disadvantage is that the super is closely involved in the subordinate's work – delegation is missing. There are many levels of management necessitating increased cost to the organization.

In a broad span organizational structure delegation becomes essential. There is a possibility of a superior losing control of subordinates. Managerial effectiveness dictates placing high quality managers. Delegation of responsibility along with requisite authority is the crux of broad span organizational structure.

Line and Staff Authority

They are identified with relationships and not departments. In line authority a superior is directly responsible for the organizational actions of a subordinate. It entails making decisions and acting upon them. In Staff authority it is limited only to the extent of giving counsel/advice. The advice given by staff authority is not binding on line authority. This is not to be confused with a **line employee** which is someone who works on any type of assembly line, manufacturing, etc.

 # Line and Functional Authority

Functional authority is the right of people in other departments (i.e., other than one's own) to control selected policies, practices, procedures, processes or other functional matters with the sole aim of accomplishing set organizational goals.

 # Delegation of Authority

The idea behind delegation is to make organizing easy. A collective effort is the key to success in an organization. Delegation of authority happens when a supervisor bestows on a subordinate discretion to make decisions in the best interest of the organization. It can be specific to perform a task or a cluster of tasks, or general, written or unwritten. It is also possible for the super-ordinate to revoke the delegated authority any time.

The **parity principle** comes into play when authority is delegated. It means that the supervisor or manager should give the employee the resources and independence to complete the task the manager has given him. The employee should use those resources needed, but no more than necessary. There should be no **dis**parity between the two, hence the name parity principle.

Unity of Command

The reporting relationship of a subordinate will be smooth and effective if it is to a single superior. If an employee has to report to more than one superior then confusion, inefficiency, lack of control and total chaos prevail. A subordinate reporting to a single superior is unity of command in its simplest definition.

Centralization and Decentralization

In centralization, all authority is concentrated at the top. In decentralization, decision making is widely dispersed. A decentralized authority, if it is re-centralized or to put it simply, if all the authority dispersed is revoked and centralized again, it is called Re-centralization of authority.

A Centralized Authority

A Decentralized Authority

Organization Charts

Functional grouping of a manufacturing organization:

Territorial grouping of a manufacturing organization:

Market-oriented grouping of an organization:

Matrix and Project Organizations

In a matrix or project organization an employee has two bosses or supervisors. For example, a team of engineers may have an engineer as their supervisor who has a great deal of experience in the field and who also manages their time and work. This team of engineers may also have an "executive" boss or supervisor who is in charge of completing a specific project. This executive will manage the team along with their "regular" supervisor while they work on and complete a project which was assigned to them. Generally, at the termination of the project, the executive manager will be assigned a new team based on the new project he or she is given.

Staffing

In organizing we have seen authority structures, broad departmentalization, delegation, etc. In other words we have a structure and we need people to fill up the structures to do meaningful jobs. Staffing, therefore, is a systematic and methodical filling up of positions in an organizational structure by identifying total manpower requirements, recruitment, selection, placement, appraisal, promotion, training and compensation. Organizing and staffing are closely linked.

Staffing

Directing

Directing = Leadership + Motivation + Communication. Directing is the process, which seeks to influence people towards spontaneous and willing accomplishment of overall organizational objectives. Let us consider the components of Directing.

Management by Walking Around (MBWA)

Management by Walking Around (MBWA) is a hands-on management technique where supervisors and managers leave their offices to interact directly with employees, observe operations, and gather information firsthand. This approach emphasizes personal contact, informal communication, and direct observation rather than relying solely on formal reports, meetings, or electronic communications.

The concept gained widespread recognition in the 1980s through Tom Peters and Robert Waterman's book "In Search of Excellence," though the practice existed long before. Hewlett-Packard is often credited with developing and popularizing MBWA as a formal management philosophy. The underlying principle is that managers can better understand operations, identify problems, and maintain employee engagement through regular, informal workplace presence.

MBWA serves multiple supervisory functions. First, it provides managers with unfiltered information about operations. Formal reports may sanitize problems or present overly optimistic assessments. By directly observing work processes and talking casually with employees, managers gain more accurate understanding of challenges, inefficiencies, and opportunities for improvement. For example, a manufacturing supervisor walking the production floor might notice that workers are developing workarounds for a poorly designed process—information that might never appear in formal reports.

Second, MBWA enhances employee morale and engagement. When supervisors regularly visit work areas and show genuine interest in employees' work, it demonstrates respect and accessibility. Employees feel valued when managers take time to listen to their concerns, answer questions, and acknowledge their contributions. This visibility can reduce the perception of an aloof or disconnected management, fostering a more positive workplace culture.

Third, MBWA facilitates problem identification and resolution. Many workplace issues are subtle and context-dependent. A supervisor reviewing spreadsheets in an office might miss safety hazards, equipment malfunctions, or workflow bottlenecks that become obvious during a walkthrough. Early problem detection prevents small issues from escalating into major crises. For instance, a retail store manager walking the sales floor might notice that checkout lines are consistently long during certain hours, prompting schedule adjustments before customer complaints increase.

Fourth, MBWA strengthens communication channels. Informal conversations during walkarounds often reveal information employees hesitate to share through formal channels. Workers may mention concerns about new policies, suggest improvements, or identify conflicts that formal reporting structures miss.

This upward communication helps managers stay connected to frontline realities.

Effective MBWA requires specific practices. Managers should walk around regularly and predictably, making it a routine part of their schedule rather than random or crisis-driven. Consistency builds trust—employees learn that management's presence doesn't signal problems but represents genuine interest. However, timing should vary enough to observe different shifts, operations, and work conditions.

Managers practicing MBWA should engage authentically with employees. This means asking open-ended questions, listening actively, and showing genuine curiosity rather than conducting interrogations or inspections. Questions like "What's working well today?" or "What challenges are you facing?" invite honest dialogue. Managers should avoid dominating conversations or immediately criticizing observed problems. The goal is information gathering and relationship building, not micromanagement.

Following through on issues discovered during walkarounds is critical. When employees share concerns or suggestions, managers should acknowledge them, investigate as appropriate, and provide feedback on outcomes. If problems cannot be addressed, managers should explain why. Failure to follow through damages credibility and discourages future communication.

MBWA also has limitations and potential pitfalls. Excessive or poorly executed walkarounds can feel intrusive or threatening to employees who interpret management presence as surveillance. Managers must balance visibility with giving employees space to work independently. Additionally, MBWA cannot replace formal performance reviews, structured meetings, or systematic data analysis. It complements but does not substitute for other management tools.

Cultural context matters in implementing MBWA. In some organizational cultures, unexpected management visits create anxiety rather than engagement. Supervisors should adapt their approach to their specific workplace, considering factors like employee preferences, organizational norms, and the nature of work being performed. In highly technical environments, managers may need subject matter knowledge to have meaningful conversations during walkarounds.

Documentation can enhance MBWA's effectiveness. After walkarounds, managers might note observations, follow-up items, and insights. This creates accountability and helps track patterns over time. However, note-taking during walkarounds should be discrete to avoid making employees self-conscious or defensive.

Modern technology has created new MBWA variations. In organizations with remote workers or multiple locations, managers might conduct "virtual walkarounds" through video calls, online collaboration platforms, or virtual reality systems. While not identical to physical presence, these adaptations apply MBWA principles to distributed workforces.

Ultimately, successful MBWA reflects a management philosophy valuing direct engagement, employee perspectives, and operational awareness. It requires supervisors to be approachable, observant, and responsive. When implemented thoughtfully, MBWA strengthens organizational performance by improving communication, problem-solving, and workplace culture.

Job Satisfaction

Job satisfaction comes from enjoying your job. There are many components that work together to contribute to that satisfaction. Each person experiences this in a different way, based on their personality. Satisfaction or dissatisfaction comes from many factors including:

- hours
- pay
- benefits
- peers
- social environment
- change of pace
- interest in tasks
- security
- need for achievement

When an employee is happy and likes their job, they are more effective in their tasks. Several problems such as absenteeism (not showing up for work), tardiness, turnover, and retention can be greatly improved if employees are enjoying their work.

Job Enrichment vs. Job Enlargement

The terms job enrichment and job enlargement are two separate elements which relate to job satisfaction. Job enlargement is related to the breadth of a job. Breadth is the horizontal aspect of a job, or how many aspects there are to it, and how various it is. Job enlargement is generally considered to occur in two different ways. The first is by enlarging, or increasing, the amount of tasks that have to be completed. An editor who previously had to get through ten pages a day now has to do fifteen, or a worker who had to package five boxes of product now has to package eight. This can improve worker efficiency, but it can also become monotonous and tedious for the worker, which is a decrease in overall satisfaction. The other option is called job rotation. In job rotation, the worker rotates or cycles through a number of different responsibilities. For example, a person may help produce products one week, package them the next, and deliver them the next.

The depth of a job relates to job enrichment. While breadth is related to horizontal elements, depth is related to vertical elements of a job. Depth is increased through factors such as growth, responsibility, and control. Herzberg focused on increasing the depth of a job in order to increase satisfaction. He believed that by increasing the job enrichment it would move workers from lower levels of satisfaction to higher levels, because challenge and responsibility are aspects of motivational factors. The main problem with increasing job enrichment is that it can become expensive. It can require changes to company structure. Employees in positions with job enrichment, with factors such as responsibility and challenge involved, often expect to be paid more.

Maslow's Hierarchy of Needs

Maslow's Hierarchy of Needs consists of the following stages from the top down:
- Self-actualization
- Esteem needs
- Belonging and love
- Safety
- Physical needs

These stages begin at physical needs. First you need to have food, water, and shelter before you can worry about other requirements. Once those needs are met you may start to think of other necessities, such as safety. You might buy a gun or move to a more prosperous and safe area. Once you are fed, clothed and safe you will want to meet needs of belonging and love through relationships. If you feel loved, you may begin to think about your self-esteem and how you feel as a person, what you are contributing. The final stage, self-actualization, you may never meet. Most people do not.

Carl Rogers agreed with Maslow's Hierarchy of Needs and was a true advocate of group therapy. He believed that each person had an idea of a "perfect person" and tried to work towards being like that person as much as possible. He believed that people needed to become "fully functioning" individuals. Rogers and Maslow were both Humanistic Theorists.

Leadership

Peter F. Drucker, the Modern Management philosopher and guru, states in his book "The Practice of Management" "…The successful organization has one major attribute that sets it apart from unsuccessful organizations: dynamic and effective leadership.…" Again, George R Terry, in his wonderful book "Principles of Management," points out that: "…Of every one hundred new business establishments started, approximately fifty, or one half, go out of business within two years. By the end of five years, only one third of the original one hundred will still be in business.…" Almost all the failures were attributed to ineffective leadership. This tells us in clear and unambiguous terms all about leadership. In other words, the core of leadership is accomplishment of goals with and through people. Every leader has a style. The style of leaders is the consistent behavior patterns that they exhibit when they seek to influence people in order to accomplish organizational goals. The style is the consistent perception of the followers/subordinates of the leader and not the leader's perception itself.

Q = Quadrant

Q1 = Telling stage where the leader perceives the subordinates maturity level as immature. Here he spells out clearly every task.

Q2 = Selling stage where the leader perceives the maturity level of his subordinates as moderate. Here he just gives what is expected and he would like the task done.

Q3 = Participating stage where the leader perceives the subordinate to be fairly matured and invites him to participate in decisions.

Q4 = Delegating stage were the leader thinks that the subordinate to be fully matured to take on responsibilities. He only gives a broad outline and leaves the execution to the subordinate.

There are despotic leaders who only demand what they want normally in high decibels, and encourage no initiative. They are task leaders. On the other side of the spectrum you have leaders who value human relationships, who are polite but firm with subordinates, encourage initiative and are willing to share responsibilities.

Many leaders **empower** their employees by allowing them to make their own decisions and / or giving them authorization to do certain behaviors to help a customer.

There are several different types of leaders:

- **Laissez Faire Leadership** is a hands-off approach. Employees are highly motivated and complete their tasks without a lot of input or supervision.
- **Autocratic Leadership** is the dictator approach. Employees are told who, what, how, where and when. Also known as the "because I said so" style of leadership.
- **Participative Leadership** is where the leader asks for and considers input from their employees for decision making.
- **Situational Leadership** is when a leader chooses the best style for the situation varying between all shades of different approaches.

Contingency Leadership

The idea that different situations call for different leadership styles is called the contingency theory. According to the contingency theory, while some types of work require an upbeat and positive manager or leader, others are more effective when a strict and regulatory leader is present. This is called contingency leadership, or in other words, it is the theory that a leader's style should suit the situation as well as the task.

One of the first contingency theories was developed by Fred Fiedler. Fiedler believed that a leader's style should change based on the leader's personality and the impending situation. His model addressed three different issues, leader-member relations, task structure, and leader power. He believed that various arrangements of these three factors would require either task motivated leaders or relationship motivated leaders.

Leader-member relations can be good or poor and refer to the extent to which the group accepts the leader. This is also determined using what Fielder called the LPC, or the least preferred coworker. If a leader's least preferred coworker was described positively, it indicated good leader-member relations and a relationship motivated style. If the leader's least preferred coworker was described negatively, it indicated poor leader-member relations and a task motivated style.

Task structure can be described as structured or unstructured. This is the extent to which a task must be done a certain way, or if the task is flexible or requires creativity. For example, an industrial worker must always produce a product in the exact same way, whereas a computer company needs to continually work on new and different products. The industrial worker is structured and the computer company is unstructured.

The final element, leader power, can be either strong or weak and describes the extent to which the leader exercises power over the employees. An example of this power would be the ability to hire, fire, and promote employees. The three elements in various combinations create either high control, moderate control, or low control situations. According to Fiedler, high and low control situations require a task motivated leader. Moderate control situations require a relationship motivated leader.

The contingency theory of leadership says that there is not one single perfect way to lead a group, but that the style of leadership should change based on the situation. Fred Fiedler believes that a leader's style should change based on the leader's personality and the impending situation.

There are three factors that influence the favorableness of a leader:

1. Leader-member relations
2. Task structure
3. Leader position power

When each of these three areas is rated highly, the situation is considered a favorable situation.

Path-Goal Model

A second contingency theory is called the path-goal model. This model was developed mainly by Robert House, and states that the job of a leader is to use structure, support, and rewards to create a good working environment which encourages accomplishing the organization's goals. The leader should be able to show the workers how accomplishing the company's goals will benefit them. The leader should also provide for task needs, such as supplies and budgets, and psychological support, such as encouragement.

Leaders may choose between four different styles, and the choice should be based on considerations of the worker's opinions and styles, and the work environment. The leadership styles are directive, supportive, participative and achievement-oriented.

In directive leadership, the leader clearly outlines what the workers are to do and accomplish, and how they are to do so. They provide standards, schedules, and instructions. For ambiguous or difficult tasks, this style of leadership can be appreciated and helpful.

Supportive leadership involves an open approach, with considerate and helpful leaders. The leaders create a pleasing work environment and look after the workers. This style is helpful in the situation of a tedious, unpleasant, or stressful job. If a job is repetitive, supportive leadership increases job satisfaction among workers. Participative leadership involves a group oriented structure. The leader asks the worker's opinions and considers their input. This style of leadership is most effective in nonrepetitive tasks. For example, a worker who watches an assembly line all day will appreciate being asked for their opinions much less than a lawyer, who has continually changing goals, or a person feels challenged by their job.

Achievement-oriented leadership involves a pattern of high goal setting and encouragement. This style involves challenging workers, and expressing confidence in their abilities. This style of leadership is most effective in ambiguous and challenging situations, and not for repetitive or simple tasks.

The path-goal theory leaders make it easy for subordinates to meet their goals. They:

- Provide a clear path
- Help remove barriers to the problems
- Increase the rewards along and at the end of the route

Situational leadership focuses on three main points:

1. the amount of leadership direction to subordinates
2. the amount of monetary support for goals
3. the willingness of subordinates to perform

Vroom and Yetton's normative leadership model is used in decision-making. This model helps leaders determine when and how much feedback from a group is required when making a decision. Who makes the decisions is factored heavily into the supervisor's leadership style. This theory states that no one leadership style or decision making process fits all situations equally.

Power in the workplace is known as a person's ability to influence peers, subordinates and events. Power is earned not by title but by a person on their own. Politics is the way that a person gains power. Politics include bargaining, negotiating, compromises, etc. To succeed in a corporate structure, you must have a skill for politics.

Some people have referent power which is also called charisma. Legitimate power is obtained through a specific position in the organization by a title. Legitimate power is the right to fire and hire others. Expert power is when someone is an expert at a certain task or in a certain area. Although that person may not have subordinates, they have power because of their expertise. For example, a web designer may have power if they are the only one in the organization that can provide for a web design need.

Vroom-Yetton Model

A third contingency model is called the Vroom-Yetton model, or Vroom-Yetton normative leadership model. This model follows the belief that every decision that a leader must make requires a different approach, each with a different level of involvement from subordinates, and it therefore follows a decision tree structure.

Using the model, the leader will consider a series of questions that will lead them to styles which incorporate different levels of autocratic, consultative, and group properties. There are two levels of autocratic procedures. The autocratic procedures involve decisions made by the leader, with little or no involvement from subordinates. The first autocratic level, AI, is when the leader makes the decision completely on their own using only the information which is currently available to them, or things which they already know.

For example, a leader must decide how to increase profit, and they decide that they are going to fire one of the employees they don't know with very well. They don't consult anyone, and just make the decision themselves based on the fact that they don't know the person.

The second autocratic level, AII, involves the leader gathering specific information from others, and making the choice by themselves. For example, if the same leader is determining which employee to fire, they may ask a number of employees which person is the worst worker. Often with the AII level, the leader may not even tell the people they ask what the specific problem is.

They still make the choice on their own, and may completely disregard the information they gather, but they do ask. There are also two levels of consultative procedure. In this case, the decision is made by the leader, but there is involvement from the subordinates.

The first level, CI, involves sharing the problem with individual employees and asking their opinions one at a time, never as a group. Then the decision is made. The second level, CII, involves gathering all the employees into a group and allowing discussion. In this way, the leader determines the opinion of the group and receives ideas and suggestions from them. The leader will make the decision based on what they say. The decision still may not agree with what the subordinates say.

There is one level of group involvement, GII. This level involves sharing the problem with the subordinates as a group and allowing them to choose a solution to the problem. When it is important that the subordinates support the decision which is made, or if the subordinates have relevant information to contribute, the autocratic methods are not very useful. However, if the subordinates do not see the problem as important or relevant, and the leader does, the autocratic methods are the most useful. It all depends on the specific situation.

Lifecycle Model

Another contingency model is called the lifecycle model, or the Hersey and Blanchard situational leadership model. The lifecycle model has its main focus on the state of the worker. The worker has high readiness if they are able and very willing to accomplish a task. Conversely, a worker has low readiness if there are incapable, inept, or unwilling to accomplish a task.

By incorporating their task behavior and relationship behavior, or the extent to which the leader is involved in the task and how the leader communicates, it states four different leadership types. If a leader has high task behavior and high relationship behavior, it is called a selling style. This style involves explaining decisions, and persuading workers.

The selling style is best used in the case where workers have moderate readiness. In this style, it is primarily the leader who makes decisions after discussion with the workers. If a leader has high task behavior and low relationship behavior it is called a telling style. This style primarily involves close supervision and extensive instruction. This style is best used when there is a very low level of readiness, such as when workers are unwilling or insecure.

If a leader has low task behavior and high relationship behavior it is called a participating style. This style involves group decisions, in which the leader collaborates and encourages the workers. This style is best used in the case of moderate to high levels of readiness.

The final style is delegating. In a delegating style, the leader has low task behavior and low relationship behavior. The leader will give out assignments to the workers and allow them to function for themselves. This style is best used in the case of high readiness, because it allows the competent and willing workers to accomplish tasks as they wish.

Each of the four styles has a distinct view, however they are all considered contingency models because they accept the premise that there is not a single type of leader, or leadership style, which works best in every situation. They all combine different aspects including work environment, purpose, and leader personality to provide models describing the type of leadership which they believe would best suit the specific situation.

Vertical-Dyad Linkages

Vertical-dyad linkage is also called leader-member exchange or LMX. Vertical refers to the chain of command, the relationship between leaders and subordinates, and a dyad is a group of two people. Therefore, vertical-dyad linkages are relationships between a leader and worker. In layman's terms this could be referred to as favoritism. Simply put, vertical-dyad linkages occur when a leader and a follower have mutual respect, trust and obligation towards each other.

Essentially vertical-dyad linkages are friendships which cause the development of in-groups and out-groups in a working environment. The in-groups receive favorable treatment such as interesting assignments, promotions and raises. The out-groups are the groups which do not share the mutual respect and obligations of a vertical-dyad linkage, and therefore are at a disadvantage. In-group workers tend to be more productive and enthusiastic. On the other hand, when the gap between treatment of in-group and out-groups becomes too large it can become a problem. Out-groups may become resentful or angry, and therefore less productive.

Motivation

William James of Harvard University did a research on Motivation. His findings are noteworthy. He found that hourly employees whose work pattern he studied could hold on to their jobs, if they performed at 20 to 30% of their ability. His studies further elucidated that workmen can work up to 80 to 90% of their ability if they are highly motivated! In other words if the employees are highly motivated their work ability jumps from 20-30% to 80-90%!

For some money can be a good motivator. For some others safety, i.e., security, job-satisfaction, congenial atmosphere, social needs, esteem needs and self-actualization needs are important. Challenge in one's job is a motivation for some people. Rewards for accomplishments are also a motivator.

Hawthorne Effect

In 1927 a series of studies began at Western Electric Company in Hawthorne, Illinois. The first study was testing the assumption that the worker output would increase if the level of light in the plant was turned up. To test the theory, they took several female workers into a separate room in the factory and tested their output against a variety of lighting. Surprisingly, output increased regardless of the light level, until it was too dark to see and then it remained constant. Why? By taking the workers into another room at the plant, they had done something inadvertently; they had made the workers feel special. Because the workers felt special they had a higher output. Experts coin the effect of this example to be the Hawthorne effect, which is where the interest in the people's problems affects the outcome, not the changes themselves.

Like any study, statistics were used to prove the conclusion of the study. Statistics, while dealing with numbers, belong to the "family" of science.

Theory X & Y

Theory X is a management approach where you believe that people dislike work and responsibility and are only motivated by money and other financial incentives. It also assumes that these people must be micro managed and supervised.

Theory Y is the assumption that where you believe that all people enjoy work, and will control their own performance if you give them the chance. These people will want to do a good job and work better with a hands off approach.

Communication

In communication there is a sender and a receiver. If the sender sends information (message) to the receiver and if the information is understood in full by the receiver, you have communicated successfully. The main purpose of communication in an organizational setting is to influence action aimed at achieving the common goals of the organization.

Principles of Supervision

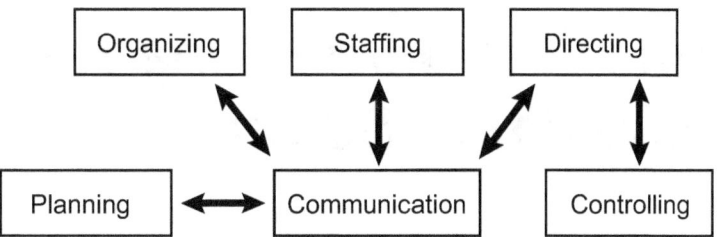

Communication is a very important factor in effective leadership and management. Not only the leaders (superiors) but also the followers (subordinates) should be adept in communicating.

COMMUNICATION PROCESS

In an organization there are upward and downward communication, horizontal communication and diagonal communication.

Communication/Information Flow in an Organizational Setting

Communication can be oral, written or non-verbal. When a message is repeated through various media, the comprehension and recall of that message is high with the receiver of such message. Simple words, using personal pronouns, adding graphs or graphics, short sentenced paragraphs, logical, cohesive and cogent presentation, and avoiding verborrhea will ensure good communication.

Group Dynamics

It is one of the training techniques used in organizations. Group dynamics deals with role playing coupled with simulation which seeks to emphasize group behavior, how groups influence decision making and how inter-group rivalry or conflicts affect organizational effectiveness. Participants discuss team development, team member hygiene, issues that are construed as disruptive and team health.

Problem Solving

Of all the skills a manager is expected to possess, analytical and problem solving abilities are most important. There are broadly three skills associated with managing. They are (1) Conceptual skills, (2) Human relation skills and (3) Technical skills.

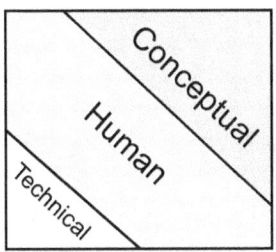

For Top Management
Less technical, more conceptual and a good deal of human skills

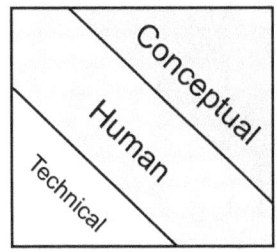

For Middle Management
More of technical and conceptual skills and a good deal of human skills

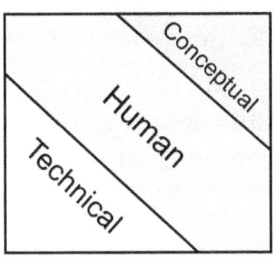

Supervisory Management
More of technical, less of conceptual skills and a good deal of human skills

(Originally developed by Robert L. Katz in Harvard Business Review - 1955)

For all the levels – Top, Middle and Supervisory, the emphasis is Human skills. "…I will pay more for the ability to deal with people than any other ability under the sun…" said John D. Rockefeller, one of the great American entrepreneurs. Managers should be ever vigilant to identify problems as they arise, analyze and track the core issue and then solve the problem by addressing the core issue and exploiting the opportunities present. After all opportunities are always there in every possible threat.

Conflict Resolution

Ask yourself, what is the conflict all about? What are the causes of the conflict? What are the possible solutions? And, what is the best of the possible solutions? Is the solution acceptable to all? Yes means you have resolved the conflict.

In an organizational backdrop, if the individual and group goals are seen as close to the organizational goals, there is bound to be an integration of goals, which satisfies all concerned.

In psychological terms conflict arises when frustration develops. The blocking or stymieing of goal accomplishment is known as frustration. In an organization conflicts arise mainly because the people in the organization have not understood their roles, assignments, tasks as well as those of their co-workers. You can educate people by having proper organization charts, authority structures, clear-cut job descriptions and job specifications, together with specific goals. Job enrichment and job rotation are also helpful.

Recruiting and Selecting Talent

There are many ways that a supervisor or manager can recruit talented employees such as:

- Newspaper Ads
- Television Ads
- Workforce Services administered by the state
- Headhunters
- Staffing Firms
- Word of Mouth
- College Recruitment
- Competitor Recruitment
- Company's Website

Once a supervisor has a qualified pool of applicants, he or she will begin conducting interviews. Because past performance is the best indicator of future performance it is important to ask a candidate about what types of projects or problems they have worked with in the past.

For example, if you are hiring someone for a high stress job, after certain needs are met, such as education and experience, you will want to ask about other stressful situations they have had and how they dealt with them. If you are hiring them to manage a team, you will want to know about experiences where they have managed themselves, a team, their timelines and other projects.

Interviewing is very important but you must also be very careful. There are laws to protect prospective employees in protected classes. You may not ask the applicants:

- Age
- Race
- Marital Status
- Religion
- Familial Status (questions about existing children)
- Disabilities

You may also not ask any questions that would lead you to any of those answers such as "What year did you graduate high school?" or anything similar.

Working with a Diverse Workforce

A supervisor's team has many different people. Each person brings their own unique problems, values, strengths and experiences to the team. A diverse workforce generally includes minorities, different genders and disabilities. It is important to remember that each employee cannot be motivated the same way. Cultures must also be considered when supervising. For example, a Hispanic worker may have different cultural holidays they celebrate with their family than another peer. Some employees may have problems working on Sunday because it interferes with their worship services or religious beliefs.

The way that we perceive other people is called social perception. Our perceptions are created by three main factors:

1. the other person
2. the situation
3. yourself

There are things that can cloud your judgment when you are trying to accurately perceive people and their motivations. These are called barriers. An example of a barrier is distrust of a new store employee because a store employee stole from you in the past.

Another example of a barrier is a stereotype. A stereotype is usually a negative term where you have a preconceived idea about a person because of their membership in a particular group or category.

The halo effect is when one person's positive or negative traits influence their other traits. An example of the halo effect would be that a worker who is always honest with their cash drawer must be a good mother as well because she is "honest" and "honest" people raise good children. Selective perception is when we limit our perceptions of others. Projection is a term coined by Freud. Projection is where we transfer our thoughts onto others. An example of projection would be an unfaithful husband who constantly accuses his wife of cheating. Self-fulfilling prophesy is when you believe something to be true and because of that premise, your action or inactions cause that to come about.

Julian Rotter originally conceived the idea **locus of control**. Internal locus of control is the feeling or idea that we can personally interact with people and our environment to influence the outcome of events. External locus of control is when a person believes that external causes, such as situational factors, influence the outcome of events. These type of people generally believe in luck, astrology, destiny, etc.

Discipline

Sometimes discipline is required to get employees back on the right track. Some government agencies and private businesses have strict rules and clearly defined consequences for breaking them. For example, many firms use a similar system comprised of:

- Verbal warnings
- Written warnings
- Suspension
- Termination

Other areas of industry such as call centers use a different approach. For example, each time an employee clocks in late or leaves work early, they are given ½ a point on their attendance. For a day they call in sick for work, they receive 1 full point. When an employee reaches 4 points in a six month time frame, they are required to fill out an attendance contract with their supervisor. If an employee reaches 6 points, they are subject to termination.

Many states have "at will" employees which means that they may be fired at any time for any reason (except for Title VII infractions which include, race, age, etc.). However, some businesses, in particular the government, has their policies so strict that they actually reduce the effectiveness of the supervisor. With some positions, so much documentation is required to terminate an employee it is almost impossible. They are required to receive a certain amount of warnings and suspensions before termination is even on the table. This is where the stereotype of a cushy "government" job got its start.

Another style of discipline is referred to as the **hot stove rule**. Just as there is an immediate response and reaction to touching a hot stove, so should there be in disciplining employees. There is also heat that comes from the stove, serving as a preliminary warning that it is hot. Also, a hot stove is always hot. Using consistent discipline offers better results.

Employee Counseling

Employees are not perfect. They can have problems with attendance, morale, drugs, anger, alcohol, attitude or even problems just completing their duties. Many companies offer counseling for problems such as alcohol or drug addiction. Other companies offer the assistance of professional counselors, psychologists and psychiatrists through their medical coverage programs. Generally, employers will NOT pay for family or marriage counseling.

Controlling & Budgets

In every organization, the top management sets out the overall company objectives, departmental targets, etc., for the managers and their team of people to accomplish during a given period of time. Managers use many tools to ensure the targeted objectives are realized effectively and efficiently. Controlling, in its larger perspective, involves the measurement of activities of subordinates in order to know whether the organizational targets are realized as per plans and if there happens to be a lagging behind, what corrective actions are to be taken to ensure 100% achievement. There are 4 elements in a control system:

Principles of Supervision

Budgets are statements of targeted results reduced to quantifiable terms. An operating budget is a "profit plan". A territory budget spells out what the target is for the territory in terms of dollars and what will be the total resources to be spent in order to achieve that quantified (in dollar terms) target. A budget is seen as a tool of control. If an organization has variable output levels, they normally have flexible/variable budgets.

Gantt Charts

A Gantt chart is a particular type of bar chart and the measuring unit invariably is time. For example, a progress chart, below is a chart which shows the progress of the actual task in comparison to what was set as the target goal. This allows the people involved to monitor how realistic they are in their timelines.

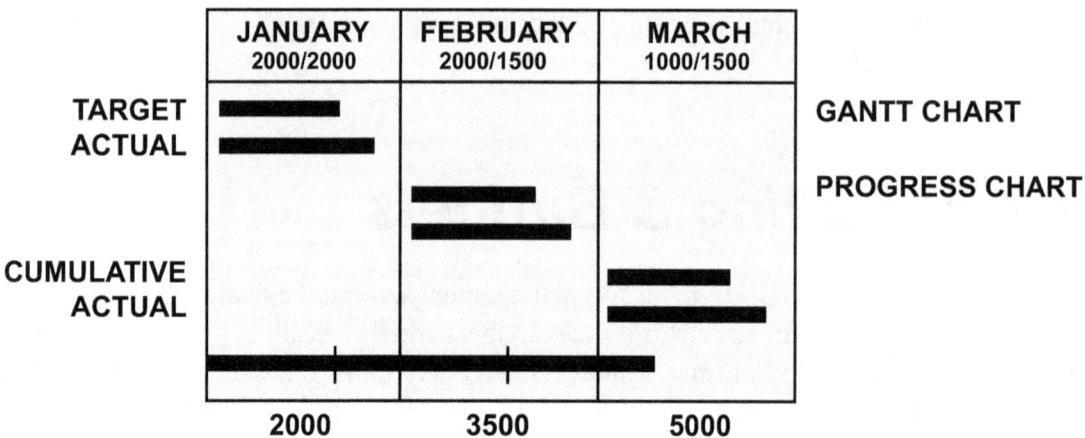

Means Chart: This is used in statistical quality control situations.

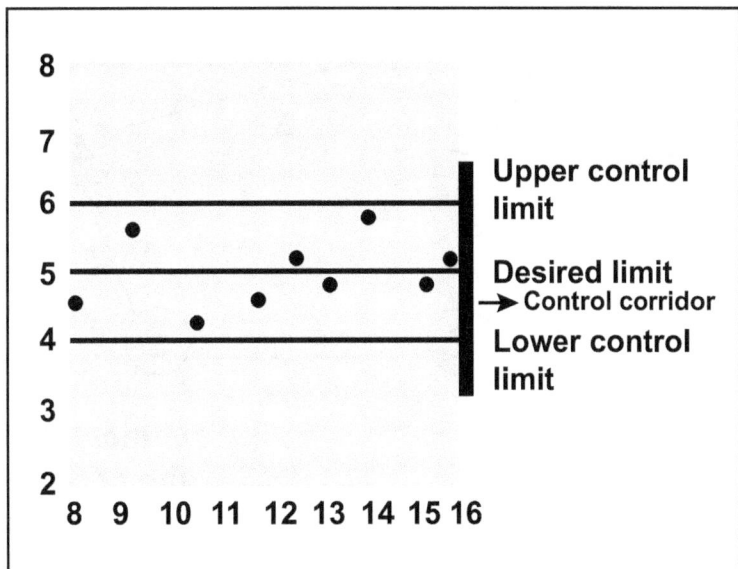

Pert (Program evaluation and review technique) and CPM (Critical Path Method):

NASA used these techniques extensively in its space programs. A project's most probable time of completion can be worked out through these techniques. Let us see an organization's budget preparation in Pert form:

Job	Description	Time Required
a	Forecasting sales	10 days
a	Market research on pricing structures of competitor	4 days
b	Sales valuing	4 days
c	Production schedules	6 days
d	Costing of production	5 days
e	Budget preparation	8 days

Principles of Supervision

Critical Path and the critical activities on the critical path

The above is a very simple pert chart. However, such charts are prepared by giving a most pessimistic time, a most optimistic time, and a most probable time. These can then be reduced into the following formula for easy calculation.

Weightage:

    t_o = optimistic time – equally likely to occur
    t_p = pessimistic time – equally likely to occur
    $4t_m$ = most probable time = 4 times more likely to occur than t_o, t_p.
    t_e = time expected

    Formula: $t_e = t_o + 4t_m + t_p /6$

You have to arrive at standard deviation $S_t = t_p - t_o /6$, which is one sixth of the difference between two extreme time estimates. Since standard deviation is the square root of any given distribution, we calculate variance from $V_t = (t_p – t_o /0)2$ using probability distribution, and thus we can say expected duration of a project.

A dummy job takes only zero time for performance but it is used to show the precedence relationship. <u>Critical path</u> may be defined as the longest path in the network. Jobs (activities) throughout the critical paths are known as <u>critical jobs</u> or <u>critical activities</u>.

Legal Issues

Risk management is an important area for supervisors. There are four ways to deal with risk:

1. Assuming the risk – setting aside enough money to pay for potential losses
2. Minimizing the risk – screening employees, network passwords, etc.
3. Avoiding the risk – avoiding certain industries (i.e., lumberjacking)
4. Shifting the risk – purchasing insurance policies

Many companies have goals regarding the number of accidents they are "allowed" to have in a certain period of time. Supervisors are awarded recognition and bonuses for having their team accident free.

TITLE VII

The final set of laws that regulate businesses are those which promote equality and safety. When it comes to equality, the primary law involved is Title VII of the Civil Rights Act of 1964. According to Title VII a person may not be discriminated against based on their race, color, religion, gender or nationality. The applications of the law are fairly straightforward, a business cannot refuse to hire someone, or do business with someone, on a basis of any of those factors. In cases where the business can prove that, for example, that the job can only be done by a specific gender then it is allowed (however, exceptions cannot be applied on a basis of race).

The Civil Rights Act also created the Equal Employment Opportunities Commission (EEOC). The EEOC was created to ensure that the Civil Rights Act was enforced, and conduct investigations in cases where there may be violations.

AFFIRMATIVE ACTION

The EEOC also helps in the implementation of programs which promote equality involving the areas mentioned in the Civil Rights Act. These programs are called affirmative action programs. Affirmative action basically describes programs which seek to reduce or reverse the effects of discrimination, as opposed to merely "not practicing" it.

The term affirmative action was first used by President Kennedy in stating that federal money used be used to "take affirmative action" in ending discrimination. Shortly after, the Civil Rights Act was passed and signed by President Johnson. President Johnson described the idea behind affirmative action by comparing life to a race. He said that you cannot take a person who has been chained up for years and, putting them at the starting line of a race, believe it to have been fair. Although the term affirmative action can be used to apply to any form of discrimination (such as gender or age), most often people consider and use it in terms of discrimination based on race or color.

Affirmative action programs have been applied not only to workplace discrimination, but also to education as well. Many universities began practicing policies designed to increase the number of minority students attending the university. While there is support for such programs, affirmative action programs have also faced a wide amount of criticism.

In one famous case, Regents of the University of California vs. Bakke, Allan Bakke sued a medical school he had been applying to for rejecting his application multiple times. Allan Bakke was white and the school had set quotas dictating that at least 16 of the applicants admitted must be of minority races. Although Bakke could prove that his admittance criteria were better than the accepted minority applicants, the minority applicants were accepted so that the school could meet its quota. Bakke claimed that this was a violation of the Equal Protection Clause of the Fourteenth Amendment. The Supreme Court ruled in his favor 5-4, deciding that although the school could consider race as an acceptance criteria, the strict guideline of a specific numerical quota was not allowable. As time progresses, businesses and universities continue to look for ways of both implementing affirmative action programs and not creating "reverse discrimination" against the minority group.

COMPARABLE WORTH

Another equality issue which aims at correcting past injustices is comparable worth. Virtually all statistics show that even today the average female worker makes only about two thirds of what the average male worker does. The theory of comparable worth is that this is a result of widespread past discrimination against women. The idea is that jobs typically held by women receive lower pay on average than jobs typically held by men because those jobs were devalued in the past. Advocates of comparable worth work to ensure that jobs typically held by women that involve the same levels of work and risk as other jobs, receive the same level of pay.

Other examples of laws promoting equality ensure equal pay for men and women working the same jobs (Equal Pay Act), prohibit discrimination based on age (Age Discrimination in Employment Act) and prohibit discrimination based on pregnancy or related medical conditions (Pregnancy Discrimination Act).

ADA

There are also many other laws in addition to the Civil Rights Act which address issues of equality. For example, the Americans with Disabilities Act (ADA) which is designed to ensure that people with disabilities receive the same opportunities for work as people without disabilities. The act applies to all government agencies and labor unions. The law also extends to private employers with more than 15 employees. Within a workplace the law can be applied to practices such as hiring employees, firing employees and promoting employees. For example, under the ADA a business may be required to install a ramp leading to the front doors to ensure that employees confined to a wheelchair are equally able to work. This sort of practice is referred to as reasonable accommodation, and it is required under the law. Another example of reasonable accommodation could be purchasing a specialized machine that could be used by a blind employee. The law does not require that any sort of preferential treatment be given to disabled employees or applicants. An employee is free to choose to hire the most skilled employee and fire the least skilled employee based on the qualifications required for a job.

OSHA

OSHA, created by the Occupational Safety and Health Act of 1970, protects worker safety and health by setting and enforcing workplace safety standards. OSHA has authority to inspect workplaces, investigate complaints and accidents, issue citations for violations, and impose penalties. The agency covers most private sector employers and some public sector workers.

OSHA establishes specific safety requirements for various industries and hazards. These include regulations on hazard communication (ensuring workers understand chemical dangers), fall protection in construction, machine guarding in manufacturing, and respiratory protection. General duty clauses require employers to provide workplaces free from recognized hazards even when specific standards don't exist.

Workplace inspections can be triggered by employee complaints, serious accidents, or targeted enforcement programs focusing on high-hazard industries. During inspections, OSHA compliance officers examine facilities, interview workers, and review safety programs and records. Employers must maintain records of work-related injuries and illnesses and report serious incidents to OSHA.

Violations are classified by severity. Willful violations, where employers knowingly disregard requirements, carry the highest penalties. Serious violations involve substantial probability of death or serious harm. Citations can result in monetary penalties and requirements to correct hazards within specified timeframes. Repeat violations face enhanced penalties.

Supervisors play crucial roles in OSHA compliance. They must ensure employees receive required safety training, have access to necessary protective equipment, and follow safety procedures. Effective supervisors create safety cultures where workers feel comfortable reporting hazards and near-misses without fear of retaliation.

FAA

The FAA regulates civil aviation in the United States, including aircraft safety, air traffic control, pilot certification, and airport operations. The agency's mission is ensuring safe and efficient use of national airspace. FAA regulations affect airlines, aircraft manufacturers, airports, pilots, and maintenance organizations.

Aircraft manufacturers must obtain FAA certification before selling aircraft, demonstrating compliance with extensive safety standards. This process involves years of testing and documentation. The FAA also certifies aircraft maintenance organizations and mechanics, ensuring qualified personnel service aircraft.

Airlines operate under FAA oversight covering pilot qualifications, flight operations, maintenance programs, and safety management systems. The FAA can ground aircraft, revoke certificates, or impose fines for violations. Following accidents, the FAA investigates causes and may issue new regulations or safety directives.

Recent controversies, including the Boeing 737 MAX accidents, raised questions about the FAA's delegation of some certification responsibilities to manufacturers. These events prompted examination of regulatory processes and relationships between regulators and regulated industries.

EPA

The EPA, established in 1970, protects human health and the environment by enforcing federal environmental laws. The agency regulates air and water quality, hazardous waste management, chemical safety, and pesticide use. EPA authority affects virtually all industries, from manufacturing and energy production to agriculture and construction.

The Clean Air Act authorizes the EPA to set National Ambient Air Quality Standards and regulate emissions from stationary sources like factories and power plants and mobile sources like vehicles. Businesses operating facilities that emit air pollutants must obtain permits, install pollution control equipment, and monitor emissions.

The Clean Water Act regulates discharge of pollutants into waterways. Industries must obtain permits specifying discharge limits and monitoring requirements. The EPA also regulates drinking water quality and wetlands protection. Unauthorized discharges or permit violations can result in substantial penalties.

The Resource Conservation and Recovery Act governs hazardous waste from generation through disposal. Businesses generating, transporting, treating, or disposing of hazardous waste must comply with strict tracking, storage, and disposal requirements. The Superfund program addresses cleanup of contaminated sites, potentially holding current and former owners and operators financially responsible.

The EPA conducts inspections, reviews compliance reports, and investigates violations. Enforcement actions can include administrative orders, civil penalties, or criminal prosecution for knowing violations. Beyond legal requirements, many businesses adopt environmental management systems and sustainability initiatives to reduce environmental impacts and meet stakeholder expectations.

FDA

Another regulatory agency which is meant to protect consumers is the Food and Drug Administration. The Food and Drug Administration, or FDA, is a regulatory agency which reports to the United States Department of Health and Human Services and employs over 11,000 people. It is the responsibility of the FDA to ensure public health and safety. They do this by monitoring many products which come into contact with people, and ensuring that they are safe, sanitary and properly labeled. Their influence includes food, drugs, vaccines, cosmetics, blood transfusions and radioactive products. However, there are things that the FDA does not regulate, including illegal drugs (which are regulated by the Drug Enforcement Agency), consumer products such as toys and appliances and the advertising of products (although the FDA does regulate advertising of tobacco and prescription drugs).

The FDA is in place to ensure that businesses and manufacturers do not cut corners with potentially dangerous products. The origins of the FDA can be traced to the Pure Food and Drug Act of 1906 which worked to counter diseases and sicknesses which resulted in the lack sanitation practices by food producing industries.

COBRA stands for The Comprehensive Omnibus Budget Reconciliation Act. It requires employers to allow employees to retain medical insurance after they quit or are terminated, for up to 18 months.

The **United States Department of Labor** is in charge of making sure companies are in compliance with federal employment laws.

EEO stands for Equal Employment Opportunity. This is a commission which investigates and prosecutes those business and individuals who discriminate protected classes which include:

- Age
- Disability
- Equal Pay
- National Origin
- Pregnancy
- Race
- Religion
- Retaliation
- Sex
- Sexual Harassment

AIDS in the workplace is a small concern for most industries. Employees who have contracted AIDS are generally not disclosed unless the nature of the job could result in injury, where the coworkers who may treat the peer would require knowledge of their condition in order to protect themselves. This is most commonly corrected by the use of rubber gloves in all situations where blood is present.

SEC

The SEC regulates securities markets, protecting investors and maintaining fair, orderly markets. Created following the 1929 stock market crash and subsequent Depression, the SEC oversees stock exchanges, broker-dealers, investment advisors, mutual funds, and public companies.

Public companies must register securities offerings with the SEC and provide extensive disclosures about their business, financial condition, and risks. The Securities Act of 1933 requires companies selling securities to investors to provide truthful information. The Securities Exchange Act of 1934 requires ongoing disclosure through quarterly and annual reports, creating transparency for investors.

The SEC enforces laws against securities fraud, insider trading, and market manipulation. Insider trading occurs when individuals trade securities based on material non-public information, violating duties to shareholders. The SEC investigates suspicious trading patterns and can bring civil enforcement actions or refer cases for criminal prosecution.

Public company executives certify the accuracy of financial statements under the Sarbanes-Oxley Act, enacted after accounting scandals at Enron and WorldCom. This law increased penalties for securities fraud and established requirements for internal controls over financial reporting.

SUPERVISORY COMPLIANCE RESPONSIBILITES

Supervisors must understand which regulatory agencies oversee their industry and operations. This includes knowing applicable regulations, maintaining required documentation, and implementing compliance programs. Training employees on regulatory requirements ensures consistent compliance throughout the organization.

Effective supervisors create cultures emphasizing compliance not merely as legal obligation but as organizational value. This involves encouraging employees to identify compliance concerns, establishing clear reporting channels, and responding promptly to potential violations.

Proactive compliance programs include regular self-audits, corrective action procedures, and continuous improvement. Many regulatory violations result from inadequate procedures, poor training, or failure to maintain systems rather than intentional misconduct. Systematic approaches to compliance reduce risks and demonstrate good faith efforts if violations occur.

When regulatory investigations occur, supervisors should cooperate fully while ensuring legal rights are protected. Organizations should have legal counsel familiar with regulatory matters and established protocols for responding to investigations, inspections, and information requests.

Sexual Harassment

Sexual harassment is a form of sex discrimination that violates Title VII of the Civil Rights Act of 1964. Title VII applies to employers with 15 or more employees, including state and local governments. It also applies to employment agencies and to labor organizations, as well as to the federal government.

Unwelcome sexual advances, requests for sexual favors, and other verbal or physical conduct of a sexual nature constitute sexual harassment when this conduct explicitly or implicitly affects an individual's employment, unreasonably interferes with an individual's work performance, or creates an intimidating, hostile, or offensive work environment.

Sexual harassment can occur in a variety of circumstances, including but not limited to the following:

- The victim as well as the harasser may be a woman or a man. The victim does not have to be of the opposite sex.
- The harasser can be the victim's supervisor, an agent of the employer, a supervisor in another area, a co-worker, or a non-employee.
- The victim does not have to be the person harassed but could be anyone affected by the offensive conduct.
- Unlawful sexual harassment may occur without economic injury to or discharge of the victim.
- The harasser's conduct must be unwelcome.

It is helpful for the victim to inform the harasser directly that the conduct is unwelcome and must stop. The victim should use any employer complaint mechanism or grievance system available.

When investigating allegations of sexual harassment, EEOC looks at the whole record: the circumstances, such as the nature of the sexual advances, and the context in which the alleged incidents occurred. A determination on the allegations is made from the facts on a case-by-case basis.

Prevention is the best tool to eliminate sexual harassment in the workplace. Employers are encouraged to take steps necessary to prevent sexual harassment from occurring. They should clearly communicate to employees that sexual harassment will not be tolerated. They can do so by providing sexual harassment training to their employees and by establishing an effective complaint or grievance process and taking immediate and appropriate action when an employee complains.

It is also unlawful to retaliate against an individual for opposing employment practices that discriminate based on sex or for filing a discrimination charge, testifying, or participating in any way in an investigation, proceeding, or litigation under Title VII.

Stress in the Workplace

Stress is our response to any change. A stressor is anything that causes us to have to adjust to a new situation or change. Adjustment is the term for what we use to cope. For example, someone who handles stress poorly could drink alcohol excessively to compensate or to escape. Strain is what happens to our bodies when we get stressed. Eustress is stress that we can use positively for our personal growth. Some examples of eustress are: getting married, starting a new school or job. Distress is stress that can have a negative effect on us. Some examples of distress are injury, problems with others, financial problems, or the death of a loved one.

We can also be stressed by our environment. Examples of environmental stress are background stressors like air pollution or noise pollution, like when a co-worker is playing their radio. You may be unaware of environmental stressors, but they are still there.

Managing stress can seem overwhelming but there are many things we can do to control it or harness it to good use. When you realize thoughts that are irrational, like worrying about things that are not likely going to happen, you can identify those thoughts and rationally discount them.

Exercise and relaxation are critical positive ways to deal with stress. Eating right will also help you deal with stress – either through the placebo effect of comfort food or by having a healthy diet, which will allow your body to be in top shape.

Managing time is also an effective way to deal with stress. Prioritize your tasks, clean off your desk, do those little things you've been putting off. These cause stress in the back of your mind, creating stress you aren't even aware of having. Some alternative techniques to relieve stress include hypnosis, massage, meditation and biofeedback. The lesser known of these areas, bio feedback is simply a process of self-monitoring through a machine the heart rate, blood pressure, etc., and learning to mentally control them.

Personnel Administration

All resources in an organization need management, i.e., they are subjected to the processes of management viz., planning, organizing, directing and controlling. Building and machinery are physical resources. Stocks, bank balances are financial resources. People are human resources. While no other resource – capital, land, machines can talk back, only human resources can think and talk back and this makes management of this resource that much more difficult.

Personnel Administration is that branch of general management which: (a) looks into manpower resources of an organization; (b) has a managerial function of planning, organizing, directing and controlling and an operative function of recruiting, developing, compensating, integrating human resources together with keeping records on manpower; (c) aims at harmonious labor; (d) aims to achieve organizational goals by integrating human resources.

The form "industrial relations" is a broader concept, which seeks to bring in harmonious relationship between labor, managements and the government of an industry.

Managing diversity is when you create a work environment where women, minorities and people with disabilities can perform and succeed on the job.

The term "labor management" normally defines the managing of manual workers of an organization. Working conditions and worker discipline together with the general recruitment, selection, compensation, etc., are dealt with by labor management.

The scope of "personnel management" is truly wider. It deals with the recruitment, selection, placement, training, compensation, working condition, etc., pertaining to all categories of personnel in an organization. Personnel and ministration also deals with generation of mutual trust, total co-operation and cohesive work force culture and maintaining cordial relations with trade unions.

Affirmative action is a detailed plan that a company makes to recruit women and minorities into positions and promotions. The glass ceiling is a term used to describe the attitudes and unwritten policies that have blocked women or any person from moving up the corporate ladder.

Performance Appraisals

An organization's current human resources need timely evaluation of their capabilities in order to be ready for any future needs. There are two sources where managers look to appraise capabilities of human resources. (1) Personnel records (which are built on the applications submitted) and (2) Personnel Appraisal ratings.

(1) Personnel records give all the data in the application together with high school, college and other educational institutional records, selection test scores, salary/wage started and changes made during the service, promotional opportunities availed, transfer effected, training courses attended, disciplinary actions, if any, recorded and personnel appraisal ratings.

(2) Personnel Appraisal: The main purpose of any personnel appraisal plan is to help the employee to know his strengths and weaknesses, opportunities and threats (SWOT) and in order to build him for meeting ever increasing job challenges. Constructive criticism and helpful dialogue are excellent guidance for the employee to gain perspective and mental maturity to perform his allotted tasks skillfully and rise in the organization ladder. Companies rate many items pertaining to an individual and we give below an excerpt which will give a good idea of this concept.

Most companies have their own appraisal methods but the data normally sought to rate belongs to any one of the elements given above.

Good companies normally rate the person on the basis of his job-performance, attitude and behavior and the call the individual for personal counseling.

There are many methods of job evaluation:

(1) <u>Ranking system</u>: In this jobs are ranked on the basis of responsibilities and duties and their importance to overall company objectives. Salary/wages are determined accordingly.

(2) <u>Classification method</u>: They define grades for requirements that are found common to various tasks on the basis of comparison between requirements regarding each task; they are classified with relevant grades.

(3) <u>Points system</u>: Requirements appropriate to each job are analyzed and quantified. Job requirements are subdivided into smaller degrees and each degree is assigned points. The total points a job gets determines its relative position vis-à-vis the job structure.

(4) <u>Factor comparison</u>: For a few predetermined key jobs, points are allotted and wage rates for such key jobs are fixed. This will serve as a guiding factor for grading other jobs. Let us see three jobs of an organization now:

Job Requirements	Maximum Points	Maintenance Person	Machine Operator	Store Clerk
Experience	20.00	10.00	15.00	5.00
Job Knowledge and Job Skill	40.00	35.00	20.00	10.00
Negligence	20.00	15.00	10.00	5.00
Working Conditions	20.00	5.00	5.00	5.00
	100.00	65.00	50.00	25.00

The above organization fixes a basic pay of say $200 for all categories per month. In addition decides to pay $2 per point as per the above evaluation in which case the 3 job-men will receive:

	Maintenance Person	Machine Operator	Store Clerk
	$	$	$
Basic	200	200	200
	130	100	50
Points Payment	(65*2)	(50*2)	(25*2)
	330.00	300.00	250.00

Collective Bargaining and Unions

Unions are formal associations of employees formed with a view to represent employees in any dialogue to bargain collectively with the management. Their negotiations with the management include improved working conditions, better wage structures, lesser hours of work, more rest periods, etc., and generally work towards establishing good labor policies. In the USA 'organized' labor is a term normally used to distinguish members of unions from employees who do not have a formal union to support them. There are blue collar as well as white-collar worker unions in the USA. Dale Yoder, in his magnum opus "Personnel Management and Industrial Relations", has given the following as the most widely accepted general policies of American Unions:

"…

1. To bargain collectively and to expand and increase the scope of the collective bargaining system.
2. To maintain and expand the security and survival capacity of unions and their ability to withstand attacks, and to back up demands with solidarity as well as economic resources.
3. To gain and maintain exclusive control of labor supplies in particular labor markets as a means of enforcing union demands for what are regarded as appropriate working conditions.
4. To improve the economic status and welfare of union members, increasing their earnings and relative shares in national income and their influence, both in employment and in the larger societies in which they are members.
5. To develop and improve the union's arsenal of weapons – programs, practices and techniques to be used in conflict and defense of the organization and in expanding its power.
6. To represent members in the area of political action, identifying candidates and officeholders who are friendly or unfriendly, lobbying and securing political concessions for unions and their members.
7. To maintain a strong organization, democratically controlled but with enough internal discipline to implement such policies as have been described above.
8. To facilitate improved member understanding of union policies and programs and increase skill and competence on the part of union officers by appropriate educational programs…"

In reality, unions are mostly a thing of the past. Although they exist in some "trade" capacities still today, they actually hinder the American worker by not giving them the power to negotiate for themselves. If you have manage union employees and you need to talk to them about their performance, you do not speak to them. Instead, you speak to the union and they speak to them for you. It adds an additional layer in the communication making it harder for businesses to manage their employees. Also, unions involve dues which the member must pay. Unions also contribute to political groups and candidates whose views may or may not be the views of the member. The member does not have control over where his dues end up.

Training and Development

Training can be considered as a program built primarily to assist employee development. There are various kinds of training:

- Apprenticeship
- Refresher courses
- Promotional training
- On the job training
- Off the job training, etc.

The specific purposes behind training are:

- Knowledge and skill enhancement
- Makes it possible to introduce new methods. Encourages people to introduce new methods thereby making it possible for the personnel to work more effectively and efficiently.
- Knowledge on safety. It provides the much needed knowledge on how to operate machines without any risk whatsoever.
- Latest techniques: Training impacts latest techniques available and makes the operator much more skilful and technique-oriented.
- Morale boosting: Promotes self-confidence of personnel as they are trained in skills, knowledge, aptitude and attitude necessary to do their job most efficiently.
- Self-actualization: It paves the way for employees to realize their full potential.

Many corporate business houses have substantial training budgets to augment and fine tune their managerial skills. On the job training for managers include:

- Planned progression
- Temporary promotion
- Job rotation
- The committee method
- Coaching

Training needs are to be analyzed before arriving at the training program. How is need analyzed? A hypothetical case study:

 ## Training Need Analysis

Training may consist of:
- Coaching
- Conference
- Group dynamics
- Idea tracking
- Managerial games
- Multimedia presentations
- Role playing
- Programmed learning
- T Group
- Workshop
- Special tuition

Organizational Development – OD

Organizational development – simply OD – is a methodical, integrated and a well thought out and well planned approach that seeks to improve organizational effectiveness. The design generally reveals solutions to problems that threaten or are already impeding operating efficiency of the organization at all levels. It may be ineffective communication, or excessive centralization, or extreme decentralization, and/or even willful apathy amounting to non-cooperation. The solutions to problems are found in team building programs, job enrichment programs, programs meant for organizational behavior modification, or simple MBO (Management by Objective), which we have already seen.

The normal organizational development process first aims to recognize the problems correctly, then diagnoses the problems, then seeks data and information feedback, then begins designing and developing a change strategy with proper interventions and then establishes yardsticks for effective evaluation of the change.

 # Operations Planning and Control

A simple illustration of Operations Management:

Operations Management can be defined as the planning, organizing, executing and controlling of an organization's total production system through optimal use of the factors that contribute to the planning and control subsystems, viz., Men, Machines,

Materials and Methods, and in the process suggesting effective improvement for the total production system.

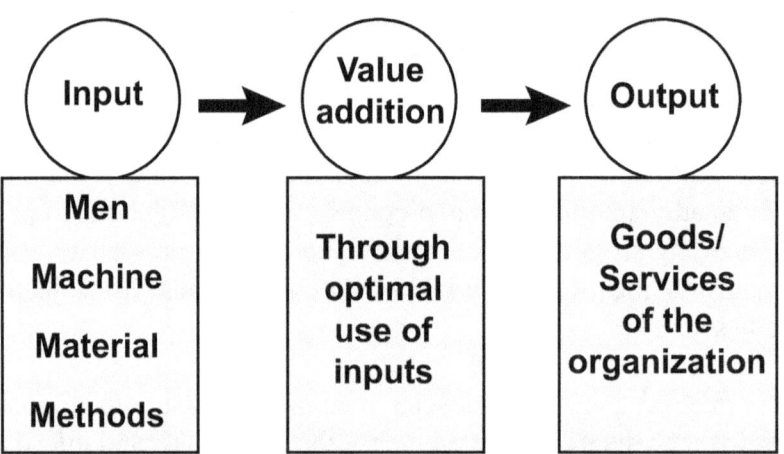

Any production system thinks in terms of excellent customer service, investment on inventory and effective utilization of resources resulting in minimal cost of plant operations. A good production control system always centers on:

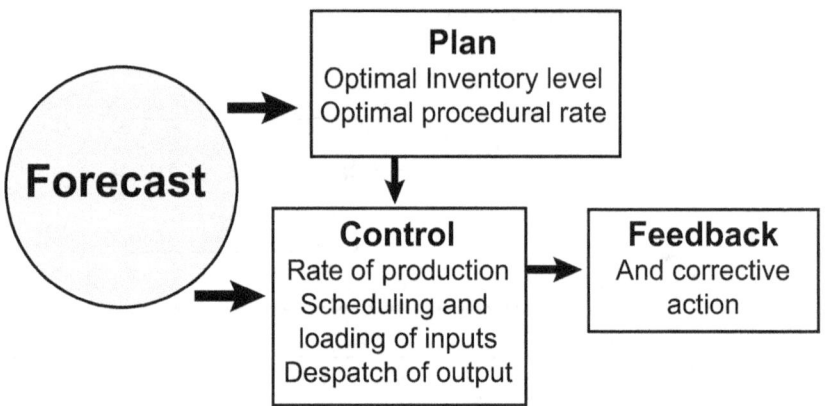

There are a few important steps in Production Planning Forecasting: (1) Preparation of essential information and data (2) Working on the forecast, and (3) Tracking the forecast.

In a factory "Lead time" means the time it takes to get an inventory item – from ordering to arrival and taking into stock. In planning production you have to take into account (a) set up time (b) production time (c) queue time (d) movement time, and (e) waiting time. A typical production plan:

Piston – 4 stroke (in pieces)

Date	Sales	Production	Inventory
Opening Balance	-	-	15,000
10/9/2000	7,000.00	8,000.00	16,000
11/9/2000	5,000.00	10,000.00	21,000
12/9/2000	10,000.00	7,000.00	18,000
13/9/2000	10,000.00	8,000.00	16,000
14/9/2000	9,000.00	9,000.00	16,000
15/9/2000	8,000.00	6,000.00	14,000
Closing Balance	-	-	14,000

Another new concept in inventory is called JIT or just in time inventory. This is the idea that you only get supplies, products and inventory right before they are needed. Wal-Mart, the biggest retailer in the U.S., is a great example of using JIT inventory. Their extensive database monitors what is selling in what store and only sends exactly what each store needs, right before they run out.

Indirect Environmental Influences (Macroenvironment)

The macroenvironment encompasses broad external forces that influence businesses but largely remain beyond individual organizational control. Unlike the microenvironment, which includes immediate stakeholders like customers, suppliers, and competitors, the macroenvironment consists of large-scale factors affecting entire industries and economies. Supervisors must understand these indirect influences to make informed decisions, anticipate changes, and adapt organizational strategies.

LEGAL ENVIRONMENT

The legal environment includes the system of laws, regulations, and judicial decisions governing business operations. This encompasses contract law, property rights, employment law, consumer protection regulations, and industry-specific requirements. Changes in legal frameworks can dramatically alter business conditions. For example, the legalization of recreational marijuana in various states created new industries while raising compliance challenges regarding federal law, banking regulations, and workplace drug policies.

Legal environments vary significantly across jurisdictions. Businesses operating internationally must navigate different legal systems, from common law traditions in the United States and United Kingdom to civil law systems in continental Europe and beyond. Intellectual property protections, labor regulations, and contract enforcement mechanisms differ substantially between countries, affecting everything from product development to hiring practices.

POLITICAL ENVIRONMENT

The political environment reflects government stability, policy orientations, and regulatory philosophies. Changes in political leadership or dominant ideologies can shift regulatory burdens, taxation policies, and government spending priorities. A government favoring business deregulation might reduce compliance costs and oversight, while one emphasizing consumer or environmental protection might increase regulatory requirements.

Political risk is particularly significant in international business. Countries experiencing political instability, regime changes, or policy unpredictability create challenges for businesses planning long-term investments. For instance, nationalization of industries—when governments seize private assets—represents an extreme political risk that has affected companies in sectors like oil, mining, and telecommunications in various countries.

Trade policy exemplifies political influence on business. Governments may embrace free trade, encouraging international commerce through reduced barriers, or adopt protectionist policies imposing tariffs and restrictions to shield domestic industries. The shift from promoting free trade agreements to implementing tariffs in recent years illustrates how political changes alter business conditions.

ECONOMIC ENVIRONMENT

The economic environment includes factors like economic growth rates, interest rates, inflation, unemployment, and consumer purchasing power. These factors influence both demand for products and services and the cost of doing business.

During economic recessions, consumers reduce discretionary spending, affecting industries like hospitality, entertainment, and luxury goods disproportionately. Conversely, economic expansions typically increase consumer confidence and spending.

Interest rates affect business borrowing costs and capital investment decisions. When central banks raise interest rates to combat inflation, businesses face higher costs for loans used to expand operations, purchase equipment, or manage cash flow. Lower interest rates make borrowing cheaper, potentially stimulating business investment and consumer spending.

Exchange rates impact businesses engaged in international trade. When the U.S. dollar strengthens against other currencies, American exports become more expensive for foreign buyers, potentially reducing demand. Conversely, imports become cheaper, benefiting businesses purchasing foreign goods or components. Companies with international operations must manage currency risk through hedging strategies or pricing adjustments.

TECHNOLOGICAL ENVIRONMENT

Technological change creates both opportunities and threats for businesses. Innovations can improve productivity, create new products and markets, and transform how businesses operate. However, technology can also disrupt established industries, rendering existing products or business models obsolete.

The internet and digital technologies have fundamentally reshaped business across sectors. E-commerce transformed retail, allowing consumers to purchase products globally while challenging traditional brick-and-mortar stores. Netflix's streaming service disrupted video rental businesses like Blockbuster. Ride-sharing services like Uber and Lyft challenged traditional taxi and transportation services.

Automation and robotics affect manufacturing, warehousing, and service industries. Automated manufacturing systems increase production efficiency while reducing labor costs, but also displace workers whose skills become less relevant. Supervisors must manage workforce transitions, providing training for new technologies while addressing concerns about job security.

Medical technology advances create new treatment options, improve patient outcomes, and sometimes reduce healthcare costs. However, they also raise regulatory questions, require substantial capital investment, and create competitive pressures among healthcare providers. For example, telemedicine technologies expanded dramatically during the COVID-19 pandemic, changing how healthcare is delivered and creating new compliance and quality assurance challenges.

Communication technologies affect how businesses operate internally and interact with customers. Email, video conferencing, instant messaging, and collaboration platforms enable remote work and global teams. Social media creates new marketing channels and customer service requirements while presenting reputation management challenges.

SOCIAL-CULTURAL ENVIRONMENT

Social and cultural factors include demographic trends, lifestyle changes, cultural values, and social movements that shape consumer preferences and employee expectations. Businesses must understand and adapt to these evolving social dynamics to remain relevant and competitive.

Demographic changes significantly impact business. Aging populations in developed countries affect healthcare, retirement services, and consumer product markets. Growing ethnic diversity influences marketing strategies, product offerings, and workplace practices. For example, businesses increasingly offer products catering to diverse dietary preferences and cultural traditions.

Lifestyle trends shape consumer demand. Growing health consciousness has increased demand for organic foods, fitness services, and wellness products. Environmental awareness drives consumer preferences for sustainable products and corporate social responsibility. Companies ignoring these trends risk losing market share to competitors better aligned with consumer values.

Social movements can rapidly alter business expectations. The #MeToo movement heightened attention to workplace sexual harassment and discrimination, prompting companies to strengthen policies and training. Black Lives Matter and related movements increased pressure on businesses to address racial equity in hiring, promotion, and corporate leadership.

Work-life balance expectations have evolved, particularly among younger workers. Businesses offering flexible work arrangements, parental leave, and employee wellness programs may have competitive advantages in attracting and retaining talent. The COVID-19 pandemic accelerated acceptance of remote work, fundamentally changing employee expectations about workplace flexibility.

GLOBAL ENVIRONMENT

Globalization has created increasingly interconnected markets, supply chains, and competitive landscapes. Businesses face competition from international firms while accessing global talent pools, supply networks, and customer bases. This interconnection creates both opportunities for growth and exposure to global disruptions.

International trade agreements facilitate cross-border commerce by reducing tariffs, harmonizing regulations, and protecting intellectual property. Organizations like the World Trade Organization (WTO) establish rules governing international trade. Regional trade agreements create preferential trading relationships among member nations.

Global supply chains allow businesses to source materials and components from locations offering cost advantages, specialized capabilities, or unique resources. However, these extended supply chains create vulnerabilities to disruptions. The COVID-19 pandemic exposed risks when factory shutdowns in China disrupted global manufacturing. Natural disasters, political instability, or transportation disruptions anywhere in the supply chain can impact businesses worldwide.

Cultural differences affect international business operations. Communication styles, negotiation practices, business etiquette, and workplace norms vary across cultures. Successful global businesses develop cultural competence and adapt practices to local contexts while maintaining core values and standards.

Energy sources represent critical global factors affecting business costs and sustainability. Fluctuating oil prices impact transportation costs, manufacturing expenses, and consumer prices. Transitions toward renewable energy sources like solar and wind power create opportunities in new sectors while challenging traditional energy industries. Businesses must adapt to evolving energy markets and increasingly stringent environmental regulations.

SUPERVISORY IMPLICATIONS

Supervisors cannot control macroenvironmental forces but must monitor them and adapt organizational responses. This requires environmental scanning—systematically gathering information about external trends and assessing their potential impacts. Supervisors should identify which macroenvironmental factors most significantly affect their industry and operations.

Scenario planning helps organizations prepare for multiple possible futures shaped by macroenvironmental changes. By developing contingency plans for different scenarios—economic recession, technological disruption, regulatory changes—supervisors can respond more quickly and effectively when changes occur.

Flexibility and adaptability become essential organizational capabilities in dynamic macroenvironments. Rigid organizational structures and processes struggle when external conditions shift rapidly. Supervisors should cultivate organizational cultures embracing change, encouraging innovation, and empowering employees to identify and respond to environmental shifts.

Productivity

Productivity is a very complex issue as it depends on a host of variables, some of which may not be easily predictable and therefore must be taken into account. The design of the job itself is a complex factor. Technology is another. Human and managerial facts lend more complexity. Add to these the external factors; you have an issue which is complex and sophisticated at the same time. In its rudimentary equation, productivity relates to the input-output ratio meant for a given time period. The constant factor of course is quality as there is no compromise on that score in any organization. If given expression, a productivity equation looks like the one given below:

Productivity = Output/Input

Suppose, a tailor, Mr. X, in a normal shift of 8 hours stitches 40 medium sized shirts. Mr. X's productivity 40/8 = 5 shirts per machine hour. The productivity here is measured in terms of units produced per machine hour worked. Increased effectiveness and total efficiency are the hallmarks of increased productivity.

Total Quality Management (TQM)

Quality of a product determines its salability. Products enjoying exceptional quality standards demand a premium. There should be a conscious effort to maintain a high quality in not only the end product, but even the methods, systems, communication and thinking of top level to the floor level employee. A good quality program includes:

- Determination of standards of quality
- Institution of an effective continuous on the job checking program with responsibilities and accountability firmly fixed
- A recording system for comparing errors vs. standards
- A method which spells out corrective action, and
- To install a program of analysis and quality improvement whenever found needed.

Checking on the production line while the job is on is a good system. However, it may not be possible to check every piece produced. Here the statistical quality methods come to help. Normally checking is done on a random basis (Random Sampling Method). The most common program liked by organizations is the <u>acceptance sampling</u> method. A sample, normally 10 to 15% of a batch from a running production line, is checked. If they find that a high majority of the checked batch quantities consistently match the set standards for qualitative accuracy, the entire batch (the balance of 90 to 85% as the case may be) is accepted. This is acceptance sampling in essence.

Today there is ISO-9000 (which tells us that a well thought out system will produce predicted quality consistently, with consistency in the implementation of the system at every stage – not only in design or production but in policies and actions of all employees), TQM – Total Quality Management (which tells us to continuously meet agreed customer requirements at the lowest cost, by realizing the potential of employees).

Six Sigma

Six Sigma is a finite, controlled, measured plan that a company adheres to in order to be as perfect as possible, with as little defects, returns, etc., as possible. This six comes from their methodology, no more than six standard deviations from the mean (average) of a statistic to their end result. What does that really mean? It means that when a product is rated six sigma, the product exhibits no more than 3.4 non conformities (defects) per million opportunities (NPMO) at the part and process levels. The methodology is broken down into two sub-methodologies the DMAIC and DMADV. The Six Sigma DMAIC process stands for define, measure, analyze, improve, and control. This is used to improve existing policies and procedures.

The Six Sigma DMADV stands for define, measure, analyze, design, and verify. This set is used to develop a brand new product or procedure.
All these concepts aim to give a zero-defect product.

The quality movement has acquired many gurus. Chief among them are: (1) Phillip B. Crosby – who always emphasized "zero-defect," (2) Dr W. Edwards Deming – who is considered the forefather of Japanese quality revolution and the thrust of his philosophy has always been planned reduction of variation, and (3) Dr. Joseph Juran who always thought and taught that quality is achievable through people rather than technique.

Work Scheduling

An effective and most efficient production control system always assigns a prominent role to work scheduling. There are input scheduling and output scheduling. In input scheduling input control is divided into: (1) Order Selection i.e., the right orders for feeding into the machines. This is based on planned production rate or customs order, or material control system. (2) Scheduling – after considering the operations to be performed on each production order, they allot times and arrive at the completion date.

(3) Loading – this involves the working out of hours required to perform each operation and then compares that factor with availability of work hours in each cost (work) center. The capacity planning vis-à-vis the machine, operations, operator, etc., tells you what would be your job flow rate. Let us see the normal scheduling steps:

In scheduling one has to: (1) multiply order quality by time per each operation. (2) To the number arrived at 1, add time of transit, and (3) provide for unexpected delays converting it to hours and add to total of 1+2.

Forward Scheduling: Starts today and works out the schedule date for each operation in order to find out the completion date for the order.

Backward Scheduling: Starts with the date on which the completed order is needed in the stores department for shipping, then works out backwards to determine the relevant release date for the order.

Business Ethics

Although there may once have been a day when a simple handshake could be considered to ensure a business transaction, business today requires far more monitoring and regulating. The study of business ethics is an attempt to apply moral principles to business operations. Ethics is closely associated with the term morality. Often the two terms are interchangeable, however there is a distinction. Morality is used to describe a person's character. It encompasses their beliefs about behaviors and can dictate how they act or respond in different situations. With morality, the focus tends to be on individuals. Ethics is the study of morality. It focuses on societal acceptance of and adherence to moral principles. Ethics focuses on the social structures which morals are a part of. Ethical principles can be considered generally accepted guidelines or expectations about the way that people (or businesses) behave.

There are three major categories of ethics, all of which come into play in the everyday operations of businesses. Three different schools of ethics are social ethics, economical ethics and legal ethics. Social ethics have to do with the way people interact with one another. For example, the morality of lying to or stealing from another person falls under social ethics. Economic ethics have to do with business and money related issues.

For example, whether or not an American company with overseas offices or factories should have to abide by United States labor laws would fall under economic ethics.

Legal ethics has to do with the actions of lawyers. Things such as lawyer-client privilege fall under legal ethics. For example, one aspect of legal ethics is noisy withdrawals. A noisy withdrawal is when a lawyer becomes aware of frauds committed by their client and withdraws legal representation for their client. They then notify the proper authorities of what they know. For example, in cases involving the SEC, if a lawyer becomes aware of fraud or illegal activities by their client they should remove themselves and notify the SEC of the wrongdoing.

However, determining ethical principles that businesses should follow is not necessarily as straightforward as it sounds. This is because businesses thrive on the ability to generate a profit. Consider, for example, a grocery store. The store purchases the groceries from a supplier. In order to make a profit the grocery store must sell the groceries for more than they paid for them. At face value this may seem "wrong" of the company to do, they are knowingly overcharging all of their customers.

However, if they didn't then there would be no grocery stores and people would have to purchase groceries from the suppliers themselves – a much more difficult process in the end. Therefore, the perceived overcharging which could be considered unethical, truly benefits everyone involved. Of course, this is a simplified example, and not all business practices can be considered in these terms, nor do they have eventual benefits, but it serves to illustrate the point that ethics is not always a cut and dry situation. What it comes down to is that business ethics is a study of the extent to which an action can be viewed as necessary for businesses to thrive, and when it becomes entirely unethical.

For example, many scandals in the early 2000s served to increase the number of federal regulations involving business, and lowered people's trust in the business community as a whole. These scandals included well known people and companies, including Enron, Tyco International, Martha Stewart, Nike and Worldcom.

Enron was created in 1985 by the merging of two large gas pipeline companies. By 2000 it had become one of the largest companies in the United States, generating over $100 billion in revenues. Not surprisingly it came as a shock when just a year later (In 2001) the company declared bankruptcy, costing shareholders and investors billions. Under further investigation it was shown that the company had been using accounting practices that were not accurate and showed the company's financial situation in better light than it was by hiding its debt. This was done by creating legal entities called special-purpose entities (SPEs) and then having them assume the debt. This created the impression that Enron had more assets than it did, and that there was a healthy cash flow because the SPEs did not appear on the balance sheet.

Another company associated with accounting scandal is Tyco International. By the end of 2000, Tyco International was a major company, bringing in around 30 billion dollars. The company had three main divisions, involving fire protection, electronics and packaging. When Dennis Kozlowski became the company's Chief Executive Officer (CEO) in the early 1990s he proceeded to expand the business into other industries, and the company soon became one of the largest producers of medical equipment as well. However, when the SEC launched an investigation of the company, it was discovered that Kozlowski had stolen millions from the company. As one example, he had purchased nearly 20 million dollars of art for himself and used company funds to pay for the art, and the taxes on it. He also threw an extravagant party for his wife using company funds. In total, it was determined that he had stolen around 75 million dollars. In addition, Kozlowski along with the company's Chief Financial Officer, Mark Schwartz, had arranged to have 7.5 million shares of stock (worth 450 billion dollars) sold without authorization, and then moved the money out of the company and into their own accounts. When the deceit came to light, Tyco International's stock prices dropped by 80%.

The scandals continued as another company, Worldcom, was forced to declare bankruptcy when an internal audit revealed billions of dollars of wrongly reported expenses. The company had been reporting operating expenses as investments. In total, the company had misreported over three billion dollars of expenses as investments. Correcting the financial statements showed that instead of growing, as it had appeared, the company was actually shrinking and in debt. Stock prices fell 99%, once again to the loss of shareholders in addition to over 15,000 people who lost their jobs.

These three incidents shook the securities markets as shareholders lost billions of dollars. The underhanded accounting practices of the three companies resulted in a widespread loss of confidence in the securities market. As a result of this loss of faith, the **Sarbanes-Oxley Act** was passed in 2002. The Sarbanes-Oxley Act tightened laws enforcing accounting and auditing practices with the intent of restoring stakeholder confidence in securities markets.

Another scandal involved Martha Stewart. Stewart built her company from a small gourmet food shop and catering business to founding Martha Stewart Living Omnimedia in 1996. She had become the iconic symbol of a homemaker and the company soon owned multiple magazines, TV programs, books and a newspaper and radio column. However, in 2001 she came under investigation for insider trading. Insider trading occurs when a person trades stock when they have information not available to the general public which influences their actions. In Martha Stewart's case, the stock in question was ImClone stock, a pharmaceutical company for which her friend, Sam Waksal, was an executive. The day before ImClone's stock value plummeted because it was not given FDA approval for a new drug, Stewart sold off nearly a quarter million dollars of shares, along with Waksal, who sold off nearly five million dollars of shares. Both were eventually convicted of insider trading and Stewart was sentenced to five months in prison and five months under home arrest for her involvement. Insider trading, along with accounting practices, is an aspect considered under business ethics.

The Nike scandal started when it was discovered that the famous athletics brand was producing many of their products in Asian factories with low wages and dangerous working conditions that would not be acceptable in the United States. The company was soon barraged with complaints, and protests were held outside of many of their stores. Within two years their revenue and stock prices had been cut in half. As a result, the company began an exhaustive public relations campaign. They accepted responsibility for the working conditions in foreign factories, and began to work with the factory owners to improve them. They established work codes, and outlined steps to achieving them. In addition, the company went around the country to different universities to restore their image in the eyes of college students.

This scandal raises many questions about business ethics. For example, should United States based companies have to adhere to United States laws even when operating in foreign countries? Also, if so, should this be universally true – or extend only to certain laws? How should child labor, safety codes and wages be addressed? Should the United States based company be held responsible for factory conditions, even if they do not own the factory that supplies their products (as was the case with Nike)? The list goes on, and all of the questions are ones that business ethics seeks to address. However, in many cases there is still not a satisfactory compromise.

Despite the many scandals of the past few decades, the evidence that better ethics actual helps businesses has become increasingly accepted. For example, some of the benefits of doing business ethically are that employees have an increased feeling of loyalty to the company. When employees feel that their company is essentially "good" they are more likely to want to continue working there. A track record of good ethics also increases loyalty from investors. If a company is doing reasonably well, and the investors feel that they can trust the company to be ethical in their practices, they feel more secure in investing in the company. On the other hand, unethical practices (as shown through the examples above) typically result in downfall of stock prices and loss of profit for the company. By extension, good ethics is therefore healthy for a company's profit. When given the choice between an ethical company and an unethical company, people are more likely to purchase from a company they consider ethical. Consider the example of Nike. Their revenues fell by 50% and people were protesting in front of their stores when they felt like the company was being unethical. Practicing good business ethics has become a way for companies to give themselves a competitive advantage over other companies in their respective industries.

On the large scale, business ethics is also important, but not all ethical problems in business occur between one business and another business or between business and the public as a whole. Some ethical issues apply to the proceedings within business, and these issues also come under the scrutiny of business ethics. For example, issues of conflict of interest, sexual harassment, nondisclosure agreements and discrimination are all addressed by the field of business ethics as well.

ETHICS REGARDING WHISTLEBLOWERS

There are numerous laws and regulations which are designed to encourage and protect whistleblowers (those who "snitch" or report of their employers misdeeds to the authorities or the media). For example, the Whistleblower Protection Act. This act protects employees of the federal government who expose incidences of waste of funds, abuse of authority, violations of laws or any other issue from any action being taken against them. If an employee feels that they are being retaliated against in some way, then they may file a complaint and have the issue taken care of.

Another protection developed for whistleblowers is the False Claims Act. The False Claims Act works from the opposite end of the Whistleblower Protection Act and encourages employees to expose efforts by companies to avoid paying federal taxes, providing false information to the federal government, conspiring to do either of those things or other acts which involve fraud towards the federal government. The act allows for compensation to the whistleblower of between 15 and 30 percent of the amount recovered as a result of their informing.

A third act with implications for whistleblowers is the Sarbanes-Oxley Act. The act has four elements relating to whistleblowers. The first is that a company must have a system of internal auditing through which an employee can file complaints. The second is that the act creates a legal responsibility for lawyers to inform on clients who are in violation of SEC regulations. The third is that the act prohibited any form of retaliation by employers to employees who legally inform about ethics violations to the proper sources, and provided the whistleblower with compensation for any legal fees. The fourth element of the act is that it allows for violators of any of the other elements can be charged under criminal law.

Moral Philosophies & Business Ethics

FUNDAMENTALS OF ETHICS

In order to form a basis from which to determine whether or not something is unethical, it must first be determined what the criteria are for something to be considered ethical. The fundamentals of ethics have been discussed and debated for thousands of years, and there are many different schools of thought which can be ascribed to. Consider, for example, if a person is judged on the consequence of their action. Does that mean that a good intentioned person whose actions accidentally result in a negative situation was acting immorally? Conversely, what if a person had bad intentions and inadvertently brought about a positive result. Does this mean that they were truly acting morally? Think instead, of if people are judged based on the morality of the actions themselves instead of on the consequence of their actions. What does this mean about a person who steals food to keep their family from starving?

Going further, what are the criteria for labeling an action or outcome as good or bad? Hedonism is one theory which claims that a person's happiness or pleasure is the only ultimate good. In essence, if something makes a person happy, it must have been a moral action. This view is contrasted by pluralists (also called nonhedonists) who believe that good is the result of many factors, and that no single action can be labeled as good. Elements which pluralists consider as measures of good are personal health, intelligence, art and personal happiness.

Even in terms of business it can be difficult to determine what is moral, immoral, good or bad. It might seem that a business's wealth or economic success could be considered a good outcome. However, there are boundaries to what a business is allowed to do to further their own position. When highly successful companies are discovered to have participated in acts that the public considers unethical it can be absolutely devastating to the company. They lose revenue and the goodwill of the public. Consider Enron for example. It could be argued that they were merely acting hedonistically and in everyone's best interest – by hiding the company's debt they were keeping stock prices high which brought money to the company, its owners and its shareholders. Therefore, they were bringing happiness to a large number of people. Yet their actions were unmistakably unethical. Clearly there is no single theory which is considered more correct any other theory. There are merely many ways of looking at situations, and many opinions about what makes an action good or bad.

The nature of what is good gives rise to, in a general sense, two different types of perspectives. These are egoism and relativism. **Egoism** is the belief that people should act only in their best interests. In other words, if it benefits the person it is the right thing for them to do. One problem with this theory, however, is that there is really no way to determine what is in the person's best interest. Should it, for example, be considered in the short term in which case many acts that would normally be seen as unethical – such as cheating, lying or stealing – could be justified, or should it be considered in the long term in which case these acts would likely prove to the eventual detriment of the individual. Another problem that arises in a business sense, is that often there are contrasting issues. For example, when the executives of Tyco International were stealing money from the company, there was an initially a benefit to them- they could live extravagant, wealthy lifestyles. However, the long term resulted in their downfalls. They spent time in prison, lost their jobs and owed the company money.

Relativism is the theory that ethics is subject to society. In other words, there really is no universal set of morals because they are determined by the state and opinion of the society in which one lives. One problem with this theory, however, is that there are some issues for which there is not necessarily a widely accepted moral opinion. Also, the theory implies that a person must follow societal norms to be acting ethically.

For example, in the United States there is a federally imposed minimum wage which is higher than in other countries. According to relativist theory it would be unethical for a business to not pay their employees minimum wage. However, if that business had branches in other countries where there was either no minimum wage or a lower minimum wage, then it is no longer unethical for the company to not adhere to the standard. This seems counterintuitive because it is the same company, however according to relativist theory the goodness of the action is determined by society and the company should feel no obligation to pay their foreign employees well.

In the case of both relativism and egoism there are cases in which the definition of goodness can be applied, however it seems that neither creates an entirely satisfactory, all-inclusive definition of what is good or bad. This is one of the challenges of ethics.

CONSEQUENTIALISM

Moving on to actual morality theories, one of the most basic terms associated with moral theories is consequentialism. Consequentialism is a broad term which refers to any type of moral theory which determines the morality of an action based upon the result or consequence that it produces. For example, a business donates money to their local food bank. This money is used to provide food to homeless families who would otherwise have starved. According to consequentialism, this was a moral act. However, by the same theory, if a person steals food from a grocery store it would also be considered moral because it has the same positive consequence of feeding people.

The most straightforward type of consequentialism is called teleological ethics. Often teleology is used interchangeably with consequentialism. **Teleological ethics** claims that if the consequence of the action is good then the action is considered moral. If the consequence of the action is bad then the action is considered immoral. Different types of teleological ethics consider how to determine whether the consequence of the action should be considered good or bad.

For example, egoism (which was described above) is considered a form of teleological ethics. This is because egoism considers the "goodness" of an action based on the consequences that it has for the individual.

MILL'S UTILITARIANISM

John Stuart Mill is known for developing a teleological theory called utilitarianism. **Utilitarianism** is a social theory which attributes an action's morality to its positive and negative consequences. It operates based on what came to be known as the greatest-happiness principle. This principle can be described as "the greatest good for the greatest number of people." This means that the good that comes about because of an action must outweigh the bad that comes about for it to be a moral action. This mindset essentially involves doing a cost benefit analysis for each situation that arises. If the benefits exceed the costs (i.e., if it causes more good than harm) then the action is moral. Otherwise the action is immoral.

For example, considering the Tyco International scandal, a utilitarian would first look at the benefits that came about because of the executives' dishonesty. Their lives were arguably enriched because of the excess funds. Then, a utilitarian would consider the negative aspects of the executives' dishonesty. The company lost revenue, the scandal caused a drop in stock prices that cost investor's money, employees lost their jobs and the executives spent time in jail. Weighting the positives and negatives against one another the most sensible determination is that the executives were acting unethically.

Mill also believed that there were different levels of happiness, and that some ranked above others. According to Mill, intellectual and moral pleasure is of greater value than contentment or physical pleasure. In essence, a large amount of pleasure from simple pleasures is not preferable to even a small amount of pleasure from an intellectual venue. For example, a college student has the choice between going to a movie with friends – which would benefit their social life and allow them to relax and have fun – and going to their classes – which would benefit them in the future by helping them understand the class better, get better grades and eventually get a better job. According to Mill, with all else being equal it is more morally correct for the student to go to class because of the intellectual benefit, as opposed to the movie.

It may seem obvious in this case that the more intellectual option is the better to choose, however the choice isn't always so simply. Consider, for example, a pharmaceutical company. Understandably, the greatest portion of the company's revenues are going to be made in more highly developed countries in which the citizens have more disposable income (income which they can spend how they choose). Because of this the company's research are marketing are both going to be geared toward products that will increase their revenue from these sources, such as diet medications or cosmetic treatments. If the companies were not to focus on developing these products, they would not be able to generate enough income to stay in business. However, in the meantime, in lesser developed regions of the world such as Africa there are thousands of people a day dying from illnesses such as AIDS, Malaria and various tropical diseases. The problem is that the price of the life-saving drugs, even when offered at production prices, is greater than the average person can afford to pay. Considered from Mill's utilitarian standpoint, the pharmaceutical companies are acting unethically because they are focusing on the less valued happiness of cosmetic, or physical, pleasures, instead of on the more important intellectual and moral happiness that would result from the development of life saving medications.

Since Mill developed this theory, it is has evolved to include two different ways of approaching utilitarianism. These ways are called act utilitarianism and rule utilitarianism.

ACT AND RULE UTILITARIANISM

The first of the two, act utilitarianism, consists of a person examining a situation, considering all the possible actions they could take and deciding which one would end most favorably for all involved. Act utilitarianism is so named because it considers the consequences of the specific action which a person is considered. It is a situation based method of determining ethics. Because act utilitarians consider actions in specific situational contexts, general rules of conduct hold little significance for them except as possible general guidelines. For example, when told that "killing is wrong" an act utilitarian would likely agree not because they find anything inherently wrong with killing, but because killing people is detrimental to society as a whole. When given a specific situation, such as self-defense, killing becomes ethical.

For example, consider a business that is based in the United States, but is considering building a factory in India and outsourcing the production of their products in an effort to increase revenue. When the company is setting up their new factory, they will have to hire employees to operate the machines. For the company's locations in the United States, they pay their workers just above the federally mandated minimum wage. They consider this to be an ethical practice because if they didn't the negative repercussions to their business would be tremendous. They would likely face lawsuits, would have a hard time finding workers and their customers would have a low opinion of them. However, in expanding to India the company realizes that the minimum wage in India is only about a third of the minimum wage in the United States. Therefore, the company offers its employees just over a third of what they pay their workers in the United States. From an act utilitarian standpoint, the company is entirely ethical in both situations. Because they consider the two situations independently of one another, the company does not have to treat all of their workers the same to be justified.

The second type of utilitarianism, **rule utilitarianism**, consists of a person considering an action independently of a situation and determining whether or not it is moral as a general rule. The rule utilitarian determines the morality of these rules based on the extent to which they result in the greatest good for society. Basically they consider the results (or consequences) of different situations to determine which is the most acceptable. This type of reasoning does not allow for exceptions under different circumstances as does act utilitarianism. In contrast to act utilitarianism, where general rules hold little significance, rule utilitarianism is entirely defined by sets of general rules. For example, if a rule utilitarian believes that "killing is wrong," then even in situations where killing would be considered self-defense, it would not be considered ethical. However, this is not to say that rule utilitarians just blanketly accept rules that are dictated by the morality of society. If a rule utilitarian is told that "lying is wrong," but after considering the rule themselves they decide, for some reason, that lying is more beneficial to society than telling the truth, they will advocate a change in the rule.

Consider now a company which follows a rule utilitarian pattern of ethics which is in the same situation as the company which follows an act utilitarian pattern of ethics. They have come to a similar conclusion about pay as the act utilitarian company, and believe that "it is not ethical to pay workers less than nine dollars an hour" for many of the same reasons that the act utilitarian company paid their workers just above minimum wage. However, when the rule utilitarian company expands to foreign countries, they would either have to reevaluate their rule, or pay all of their employees, no matter what country they are in, the same amount to be acting ethically. Of course, if the company's rule was that "it is not ethical to pay workers less than minimum wage" then they could lower the pay for employees in countries with a low minimum wage.

Thus far, all of the different theories discussed have been consequential, or based upon consequences. There are also many moral theories which fall under the category of nonconsequential ethics. These types of ethical theories do not believe that the consequence of an action is the most important factor in determining its morality, as in consequentialism, but rather consider certain actions to be inherently moral, and others to be inherently immoral.

DEONTOLOGY

One type of nonconsequential ethics is deontology. **Deontological ethics** is based around the idea of duty ("deon" derives from the Greek for duty). In contrast to utilitarianism, in deontology it would be considered immoral for a person to harm another even if it resulted in a greater benefit to society. Deontologists claim that there are things that regardless of consequence a person should or should not do. Deontologists consider the rights of the individuals involved as well as the intentions of an action in determining its morality. For example, if a worker in a company which produced radioactive materials were exposed to the radiation due to poor safety practices by the company, a deontological minded company would feel obligated to increase safety measures at any cost, even bankruptcy. In contrast, a utilitarian company would consider whether the life of the employee was worth the financial stability of the company.

KANTIAN ETHICS

One type of the most well-known types of deontological theory is Kantian ethics. The philosophy of Kantian ethics was developed by Immanuel Kant. Kant believed that the sole indicator of morality was the person's motivation for performing an action. The question that follows is what makes a motive good or bad. Many of the moral theories that have been discussed so far equate a moral act with its ability to generate happiness - either for the person performing the act or for others or for society as a whole. However, Kant completely separated morality and happiness. He believed that happiness was more a result of luck than it was a result of any choices that a person could make. He believed that to be considered good, a motive would need to be both unconditional and universal. For example, say that a person is motivated to steal from a store because they are hungry. Their motivation cannot be universalized. If every person were to act the same way as the person who stole, then the stores would have to close down because they would not be able to make a profit. Therefore, the motive is immoral.

According to Kant, there is only one truly good motive – good will, which Kant defines as acting out of a sense of duty. Because good will is the only good motive, the only actions that are moral are those which are performed out of a sense of duty, or feeling that it is the "right" thing to do. For example, donating money to a charity because you feel bad for the people it supports would not be moral. However, donating money because you feel that it is what you should do is moral.

Kant is most famous for his development of what is called the categorical imperative. Essentially the categorical imperative is just a method for testing a set of maxims by which people should live. Kant believed that people should create sets of maxims, or rules which dictate their actions, through which they consider all their actions and choices. The categorical imperative consists of two "tests." These two tests are just the conditions which were described above - a maxim must be unconditional and universal.

That a maxim must be unconditional means that it cannot be self-contradictory nor have exceptions. To carry out this test the maxim must be generalized. For example, if a person decides to enter into a contract, with no intention of fulfilling their end of the deal, the generalization would be that all people can enter into contracts with no intention of fulfilling their ends of the deals. This maxim would therefore not pass the unconditional test because it is self-contradictory. If everyone entered into a contract and didn't fulfill their end of the deal then no one would enter into contracts because they would hold no meaning.

Another example which fails the unconditional test would be false advertising. If a company advertises a product in a purposefully misleading way, the generalization would be that all companies should engage in false advertising. However, if no companies were advertising truthfully then people would not pay any heed to advertising and the purpose would be defeated. Therefore, under Kantian ethics false advertising is immoral because it is not unconditional. In the case of false advertising there are actually federal laws which prevent companies from being unethical. The Federal Trade Commission Act was passed in 1914 and, in addition to creating the Federal Trade Commission, it dictated that advertising cannot be deceptive or unfair, and it must be backed up by evidence. This policy of honest advertising is referred to as truth in advertising.

The second condition – that a maxim must be universal – basically means that if you applied the principle universally it has to create conditions that a person would be willing to live under (or that a person would choose to live under). This rule comes into play for maxims that may be unconditional, but would be detrimental to society if they were considered acceptable on a wide scale. For example, a person may say that they will not help anyone who does not have the ability to compensate them, even though the cost to themselves would be minimal. The generalization would be that no person would help another who does not have the ability to compensate them, even at minimal costs to themselves. It is feasible that the world could operate under these conditions; therefore, the maxim passes the test of being unconditional. However, if the maxim were universalized it would create a world where people do not donate to charity or do not help a person who is stranded on the side of the road. Also, if people only helped people that could compensate them, it would create a world where people would not call the fire station when their neighbor's house was on fire - it does not directly benefit them to help their neighbor. Most likely a person would not chose to live in a world like this, and therefore the maxim does not pass the second test.

Kant described maxims, or **categorical imperatives**, as distinct from what he called hypothetical imperatives. While maxims are universal, hypothetical imperatives are more situation specific. Hypothetical imperatives are essentially instructions on how to either achieve or not achieve a goal. Usually they are in the form of if-then statements. For example, if a person's goal was that they wanted to do well on an exam, a hypothetical imperative that they may follow would be "if I want to do well on the exam then I should study." Alternatively, if a person's goal were to not get arrested, their hypothetical imperative may be "if I do not want to get arrested, then I should not break the law." Kant did not believe that hypothetical imperatives could be used to measure morality. This is because they are, by definition, attached to a goal. Under Kantian ethics, the morality of an action is not judged based on the result of the action. In addition, if the hypothetical imperative did not apply to a person, such as if they didn't really care if they passed the exam or got arrested, then they would simply ignore it. For this reason Kant asserts that the categorical imperative version (such as "don't break the law") is a better judgment of morality than the hypothetical imperatives.

Another type of imperative which has become a part of Kantian ethics is called the practical imperative. The practical imperative simply states that people are to treat humanity as an end and never as a means. The practical imperative is really just a specific categorical imperative. It is designed to prevent exploitation. If a person considers the betterment of humanity as the acceptable result of a maxim, then they will not adopt any maxims which are detrimental to humanity as a whole.

For example, the **Truth in Lending Act (TILA)** is one regulation which prevents lenders from exploiting those that they lend money to (and by extension from violating the practical imperative). The Act requires that certain information be disclosed when a person is applying for a loan or credit card so that they can more easily compare different options. For example, TILA requires that things like the finance charge, schedule of payments and annual percentage rates (APR) are disclosed. It also requires that it is disclosed when a credit card has a yearly or monthly fee attached to it. This prevents consumers from exploitation which arises from a lack of information about their transactions.

VIRTUE ETHICS

An additional ethical theory to consider is virtue ethics. The theory of virtue ethics is that as people develop and interact with one another they acquire a certain moral character. They decide which things they think are moral and immoral. People will then act according to what they believe is moral. They will be honest if they find honesty moral, and they will be kind if they find kindness moral.

COMPARING ETHICAL PERSPECTIVES

Because of all of the different ways to consider ethics, people given the same situation can often chose different courses of action, and for many different reasons. Consider, for example, a salesperson who distributes tasers to policemen across the country. Assume that the salesperson knows that the tasers in a particular batch have been manufactured incorrectly and have a 2% chance of backfiring on the user. The FBI has just ordered a new shipment and the salesperson must decide whether they should inform the FBI about the defect, or ignore it and sell the tasers anyway.

If the salesperson considers the situation from an egoist standpoint, he will consider the consequences to himself if he informs the FBI or doesn't. He would most likely consider the fact that if he informed the FBI about the defect, he would most likely lose the sale. His income would decrease and his reputation would be ruined. However, if he chooses not to inform the FBI the chances of an officer's taser misfiring is fairly low, and they may never even have a problem. Even if they did, the consequence to the salesperson would be minimal – it would probably get written off as a random accident. Therefore, the salesperson would most likely not inform the FBI about the defect and would continue with the sale.

If the salesperson considered the situation from a rule utilitarian standpoint, they would consider whether it were ethical as a general rule to sell defective products. They would consider all of the outcomes in situations where defective products were sold. Most likely, they would determine that as a general rule, it would be unethical to sell defective products, and therefore would inform the FBI of the defect.

If the salesperson considered the situation from an act utilitarian standpoint, they would consider the outcome for all involved. The salesperson knows that if they go through with the sale, it is possible that the defect puts a policeman's life in danger if the taser misfires. However, they would consider that the chance of a misfire was remote. Also, if they inform the FBI of the defect and the FBI cancels their order, they would have to use time and resources to find another vendor, and the policemen would be entirely without tasers until they could do so. Therefore, knowing the benefit and costs to both themselves and the FBI, the person may choose to continue with the sale because it is more favorable for them and the FBI to just get through with the sale.

If the salesperson considered the situation from a Kantian standpoint, they would generalize the situation into a maxim. For example, "I will sell defective products." To test the maxim they would consider whether it is unconditional. If everyone sold defective products, then no one would want to buy products from other people, so the maxim is not unconditional. Therefore, the salesperson would determine that it would be unethical to continue with the sale, and inform the FBI of the defect.

It is also important to consider, along with different moral theories, the way that these theories can influence decision making in business. Often people adhere to different ethical and behavioral standards in their personal and professional lives. For example, people wait until they are acknowledged to talk, or in the case of school they raise their hand to talk, though they typically wouldn't do so in home situations.

KOHLBERG'S MODEL OF COGNITIVE MORAL DEVELOPMENT

Lawrence Kohlberg, a psychologist, developed a theory which outlined six stages which he believed that people went through as their mental and moral understanding developed. This theory is called Kohlberg's Model of Cognitive Moral Development. Kohlberg used the theories of Jean Piaget as a basis for his model Piaget studied the way that children learned as they got older. Kohlberg extended Piaget's model to apply to moral behaviors as well. He believed that all people progressed through the stages, one at a time in order (no stages could be skipped). Kohlberg's model looks at the motivations behind a person or businesses actions.

In stage one of Kohlberg's Model of Cognitive Moral Development a person is motivated by avoidance of punishment. Kohlberg believed this to be the most immature reason to do something. For example, a child does their chores to avoid being grounded.

Their understanding is that doing their chores is the right thing to do because it saves them from punishment. This doesn't just apply to children however. Another example of motivation in the first stage is people who don't speed because they do not want to get a ticket. The behavior – driving slower then they prefer – is brought on by a want to avoid the punishment of the ticket. The reasoning, therefore, is that driving the speed limit must be the right thing to do because it helps to avoid the punishment of a ticket.

In the sphere of business the first stage describes a business which acts appropriately in an attempt to avoid the negative ramifications of breaking the law. For example, a company would prefer to pay their workers less than minimum wage, however if they were to do so their employees would most likely sue them for the difference in wages. Therefore, companies who require workers that are relatively unskilled, or easily replaceable, would typically follow a stage one mentality in paying their workers.

In stage two a person is motivated through seeking rewards. This isn't to say that they don't ever think about the punishments that may come as a result of their actions, but the primary reason that they make the choices that they do is because they know that they will benefit from it. For example, instead of a person driving slowly because they are afraid of getting a ticket, a person in stage two of Kohlberg's model would chose to not speed because they want the lower rates of car insurance that will result from not having any tickets.

In business terms this stage could be used to describe, for example, companies that donate large amounts of money to charity only because it is a tax write off. This is not to say that what they are doing is in some way wrong, just that their primary motivation is seeking benefits. The reasoning being, therefore, that donating money is the right thing to do because it has a positive consequence for the business.

Another example is companies that require highly specialized and skilled workers. Skilled workers get paid more than unskilled workers (such as in the stage one example) because they are less easily replaceable. Therefore, companies will offer such workers more and more money so that they will chose to work for them instead of another company. This behavior isn't brought on by an effort to be generous to the worker or to make their lives better and more fulfilling. Rather, the behavior is induced by the company's need for the worker, and therefore it is a stage two mentality. The company is paying the worker more because it benefits them in the end.

In stage three a person is motivated by how they believe their actions will be perceived, and also by how it benefits or hurts other people. In this stage a person considers whether their action will gain them approval from others or heighten their status in other's eyes. For example, instead of a person not wanting to get a speeding ticket because it would heighten their insurance premiums, an individual in stage three would not want to get a speeding ticket because of what their friends and family would think of them if they did. At this level, the person would consider what they did to be wrong or immoral because it lowered their peer's opinion of them.

Businesses that deal with nuclear waste, for example, must be very careful of how they deal with that waste so that people will not develop a negative opinion of them. A negative public opinion could make it harder for the company to get approval for their business operations. Obviously it would be cheaper for companies to just dump the waste somewhere, but that would be dangerous to the surrounding areas. If a company chooses to dispose of their nuclear waste properly only because they worry about the negative opinions that customers would have if they did not (and not because they had any particular care for the negative impacts to the people or environment), they would be in stage three. By their reasoning, disposing of nuclear waste improperly is wrong because it generates negative opinions about the company.

Another example would be if an assistant manager was told by the manager of a factory that the output was not great enough, and that the machines needed to start running faster, forcing the workers to produce more products quickly. The assistant manager (if his reasoning followed the stage three level of cognitive moral development) would consider not only the consequences for himself if he did or did not obey the order, but whether the increased production would benefit the workers and if it would make them happier (such as if it increased their wages) or if it would merely make them angry with him.

In stage four, a person is motivated by the demands of authority figures. People in this stage will feel that something is right because they are told to do it by a person in charge (or that it is wrong because they are told not to do it). Stage four naturally leads to people following the laws because they believe that it is inherently right to follow the laws and inherently wrong to break them. For example, a person would want to avoid getting a speeding ticket not because they cared in any way about the consequences, but because they just feel that it is wrong to speed.

This stage describes a business which just follows the laws. For example, instead of the company from the stage three example disposing of their nuclear waste properly because they worry about public opinion of them, from a stage four standpoint the company would dispose of the nuclear waste properly because it is the law to do so.

An assistant manager who was told by the manager of a factory to increase production would, from a stage four standpoint, do so without really questioning it. This illustrates the main difference between stage three and stage for of Kohlberg's Model of Cognitive Moral Development. Although in both stages morality is derived from sources other than the person directly, in stage three the focus is on more of a collective opinion and in stage four the focus is on authority figures.

In stage five a person is motivated by an obligation to society. They recognize that other people have their own opinions and viewpoints, and are concerned with the affect that their actions have on society. The person works to achieve happiness for all, and learns to compromise. In this stage particularly, the idea of a social contract (a balancing between rights and responsibilities held by individuals that is to the benefit of all people) becomes relevant. For example, in stage five a person would choose not to speed because they feel that it is their obligation to drive safely. They don't want to be responsible for an accident which could harm another person.

Returning to the nuclear waste example, the company would choose to dispose of their nuclear waste properly, not because of any outside source's opinion, but because they felt obligated to society to ensure that no one was harmed by the nuclear waste that they had generated. The company would consider it to be their responsibility to act for the safety of society and the environment.

In stage six a person believes in adherence to universal ethical principles. A person's actions are taken out of a personal feeling and opinion of morality and correctness. This stage is characterized by people being ruled by their consciences. Kohlberg believed that few people, if any, achieved this degree of moral development.

Kohlberg's six stages are often broken down into three, more general, levels. The first level is called pre-conventional morality. This level encompasses the first two stages. Therefore, decisions in this stage are made through simple understanding of punishment and reward systems. The person is concerned with their immediate interests. The second level is called conventional morality. This level encompasses stages three and four. In this stage a person's main focus is on fitting societal norms and meeting expectations. The final level is post conventional. In the post conventional stage a person is ruled by conscience instead of society. This breakdown illustrates that as a person moves through the six stages, their moral development advances from a morality determined through self-interest, to one determined by society, to one determined by the individual.

Gross Domestic Product (GDP)

Gross Domestic Product (GDP) measures the total monetary value of all finished goods and services produced within a country's borders during a specific time period, typically calculated quarterly and annually. GDP serves as the primary indicator of economic size and health, influencing business decisions, government policies, and international comparisons. Supervisors should understand GDP because it reflects the economic environment in which businesses operate.

GDP can be calculated through three equivalent approaches: the production approach (summing value added at each production stage), the income approach (summing all incomes earned in production), and the expenditure approach (summing all spending on final goods and services). The expenditure approach is most commonly cited and divides GDP into four main components: consumption, investment, government spending, and net exports.

Consumption represents household spending on goods and services, including durable goods (cars, appliances), nondurable goods (food, clothing), and services (healthcare, education). In the United States, consumption typically accounts for about 70% of GDP, making consumer spending the largest economic driver. When consumers feel confident about economic conditions and their financial situations, they increase spending, stimulating economic growth. Conversely, during recessions or periods of uncertainty, consumers reduce spending, slowing growth.

Investment includes business spending on capital equipment, structures, and inventories, plus residential construction. Business investment reflects corporate confidence in future economic conditions. When businesses expect growing demand, they invest in expanding capacity, purchasing equipment, and hiring workers. During downturns, businesses defer investment, waiting for clearer economic signals. Inventory changes can provide early indicators of economic shifts—building inventories suggests businesses anticipate increasing sales, while reducing inventories may signal weaker expected demand.

Government spending encompasses federal, state, and local government purchases of goods and services, including defense spending, education, infrastructure, and public employee salaries. Transfer payments like Social Security and unemployment benefits are excluded from GDP calculation because they don't represent production of new goods or services. Government spending can stabilize economies during recessions through countercyclical fiscal policy, though the effectiveness and appropriateness of such interventions remain debated.

Net exports equal exports minus imports. When a country exports more than it imports, net exports contribute positively to GDP. Trade deficits, where imports exceed exports, reduce GDP. The United States has run persistent trade deficits for decades, partially reflecting the dollar's role as global reserve currency and American consumers' strong demand for imported goods.

GDP growth rates indicate economic expansion or contraction. Positive GDP growth signifies an expanding economy producing more goods and services, typically accompanied by job creation and rising incomes. Negative GDP growth indicates economic contraction. Two consecutive quarters of negative GDP growth constitute a technical recession, though the National Bureau of Economic Research officially determines recession periods using broader criteria.

Real GDP adjusts for inflation, allowing meaningful comparisons across time periods. Nominal GDP uses current prices and can increase simply due to price inflation without actual production increases. Real GDP uses constant prices from a base year, isolating changes in production quantity from price changes. When evaluating economic growth, real GDP provides more accurate measures of actual economic expansion.

GDP per capita divides total GDP by population, providing a rough measure of average living standards. Countries with high GDP per capita generally enjoy higher material living standards than those with lower GDP per capita. However, GDP per capita is an average—it doesn't reflect income distribution or inequality within countries.

GDP has significant limitations as a measure of economic welfare. It excludes non-market activities like household production and volunteer work. Environmental degradation isn't subtracted from GDP—in fact, cleanup activities increase GDP even though they address damages caused by earlier production. GDP doesn't measure income distribution, quality of life, leisure time, or overall happiness. A country could have rising GDP while most citizens experience declining living standards if growth concentrates among the wealthy.

The underground economy—illegal activities and unreported legal income—escapes GDP measurement, potentially understating true economic activity. Different countries have varying informal economy sizes, complicating international comparisons.

For businesses and supervisors, GDP trends provide context for strategic planning. Strong GDP growth typically creates opportunities for business expansion, increased sales, and hiring. Companies may invest in new facilities, develop new products, or enter new markets when economic growth appears sustainable.

Declining or negative GDP growth signals economic headwinds requiring defensive strategies. Businesses may reduce inventory, delay capital investments, implement cost controls, or reduce workforce. Consumer-facing businesses are particularly sensitive to GDP changes affecting household incomes and spending.

Industry-specific GDP components offer more targeted insights. Retail businesses closely monitor consumption trends. Construction and manufacturing companies track investment spending. Defense contractors follow government spending patterns. Export-oriented businesses analyze international GDP growth and exchange rates.

Central banks use GDP data to guide monetary policy. The Federal Reserve aims to promote maximum employment and price stability, adjusting interest rates based partly on GDP growth rates. Strong growth with rising inflation may prompt interest rate increases to prevent overheating. Weak growth may lead to rate reductions to stimulate economic activity.

GDP forecasts help businesses plan. Economists and organizations produce GDP growth projections based on current conditions and expected developments. While forecasts aren't perfectly accurate, they provide frameworks for scenario planning and risk assessment.

International GDP comparisons reveal relative economic sizes and growth rates. The United States has the world's largest GDP in nominal terms, while China ranks second. However, purchasing power parity (PPP) adjustments, which account for different price levels across countries, can alter rankings. GDP comparisons help businesses identify growing markets, assess competitive threats, and allocate resources globally.

NAFTA and GATT

International trade agreements establish frameworks governing commerce between nations, reducing barriers and creating more predictable business environments. Two historically significant agreements—the North American Free Trade Agreement (NAFTA) and the General Agreement on Tariffs and Trade (GATT)—shaped modern global trade architecture. Understanding these agreements helps supervisors navigate international business environments and appreciate trade policy impacts.

GENERAL AGREEMENT ON TARIFFS AND TRADE (GATT)

GATT, established in 1947 among 23 countries, provided the foundation for the post-World War II international trading system. Created during negotiations that failed to establish a comprehensive International Trade Organization, GATT served as an interim arrangement that lasted nearly 50 years. Despite its provisional nature, GATT substantially liberalized international trade and promoted economic recovery and growth.

GATT's primary purpose was reducing tariffs and other trade barriers through multilateral negotiations. Member countries participated in successive negotiation "rounds," each achieving further tariff reductions and addressing broader trade issues. The Kennedy Round (1964-1967) achieved significant tariff cuts. The Tokyo Round (1973-1979) addressed non-tariff barriers like quotas and government procurement policies. The Uruguay Round (1986-1994), the most comprehensive, addressed services, intellectual property, and agriculture while creating GATT's successor organization.

GATT operated on several fundamental principles. The most-favored-nation (MFN) principle required countries to extend to all GATT members the best trade terms they offered any single member, preventing discriminatory trade practices. If Country A reduced tariffs on automobiles from Country B, it had to offer the same tariff reduction to all GATT members. This promoted multilateral trade liberalization rather than preferential bilateral arrangements.

National treatment required countries to treat imported products no less favorably than domestically produced goods once they cleared customs. Countries couldn't impose discriminatory taxes or regulations on imports compared to domestic products. This prevented countries from using domestic regulations to protect local industries after reducing tariffs.

GATT permitted exceptions to these principles. Countries could form customs unions or free trade areas that eliminated tariffs among members while maintaining external tariffs. The European Economic Community (predecessor to the European Union) formed under this exception. GATT also allowed temporary trade restrictions to address balance of payments difficulties or protect developing industries in less developed countries.

Dispute resolution under GATT involved consultation and negotiation among member countries. When trade disputes arose, GATT panels heard cases and issued recommendations. However, enforcement mechanisms were weak—losing parties could block adoption of panel reports. This limitation reduced GATT's effectiveness in resolving conflicts.

The Uruguay Round (1986-1994) transformed international trade governance. Negotiations expanded beyond goods to include services and intellectual property. The resulting agreements created the World Trade Organization (WTO) in 1995, replacing GATT with a permanent institution having stronger enforcement mechanisms and broader authority.

The WTO inherited GATT's principles while expanding coverage. Services trade now fell under the General Agreement on Trade in Services (GATS). The Agreement on Trade-Related Aspects of Intellectual Property Rights (TRIPS) established minimum standards for protecting patents, copyrights, and trademarks internationally. Dispute settlement procedures became binding—countries couldn't block rulings against them, and the WTO could authorize trade sanctions against violators.

NORTH AMERICAN FREE TRADE AGREEMENT (NAFTA)

NAFTA, implemented in 1994, created a free trade zone among the United States, Canada, and Mexico. The agreement eliminated most tariffs and trade barriers between these countries, creating one of the world's largest trading blocs. NAFTA represented a significant expansion of the earlier Canada-U.S. Free Trade Agreement and marked Mexico's integration into North American trade systems.

NAFTA's primary goal was eliminating tariff and non-tariff barriers to trade and investment. Tariffs on most goods were immediately eliminated or phased out over transitional periods, some extending 15 years for sensitive products. Non-tariff barriers like import licenses and quotas were similarly reduced or eliminated.

The agreement covered more than tariff elimination. NAFTA included provisions on services trade, intellectual property protection, investment, and government procurement. U.S. and Canadian companies gained expanded access to Mexican markets and vice versa. Foreign investment protections gave companies greater confidence investing across borders.

NAFTA established dispute resolution mechanisms for trade conflicts between member countries and between investors and governments. These procedures provided alternatives to domestic courts, potentially offering more neutral forums for resolving conflicts.

Supporters argued NAFTA would increase trade, create jobs, and promote economic growth by allowing companies to specialize and achieve economies of scale across larger markets. Lower tariffs would reduce consumer prices. Investment provisions would facilitate cross-border capital flows, promoting development, particularly in Mexico.

Critics raised concerns about job losses in the United States and Canada as companies moved production to Mexico to access lower-cost labor. Labor unions particularly opposed NAFTA, fearing manufacturing job migration. Environmental groups worried that weaker Mexican environmental enforcement would create pollution havens and pressure for regulatory rollback in other countries. Agricultural interests expressed concern about competing with Mexican farmers.

NAFTA's impacts have been extensively studied and debated. Trade between the three countries increased substantially—trilateral trade more than tripled from NAFTA's implementation through 2020. However, attributing specific employment or economic changes to NAFTA is complex because numerous other factors affect economies simultaneously, including technological change, global economic conditions, and other policy changes.

Some U.S. manufacturing jobs likely moved to Mexico, particularly in industries like automobiles and electronics where Mexican labor costs provided advantages. However, total U.S. employment generally grew during most of NAFTA's existence, though not necessarily in manufacturing. Technological change and automation arguably had larger impacts on manufacturing employment than trade policy.

Mexican agricultural sectors experienced disruption as U.S. agricultural exports, particularly corn, entered Mexican markets at lower prices due to U.S. agricultural subsidies and economies of scale. This affected Mexican small farmers, contributing to rural-urban migration.

NAFTA created complex supply chains where products crossed borders multiple times during production. For example, automobile manufacturing integrated across all three countries, with parts and components moving between facilities for different production stages. This integration created efficiencies but also vulnerabilities to disruptions at any point in the supply chain.

In 2018-2020, NAFTA was renegotiated and replaced by the United States-Mexico-Canada Agreement (USMCA). The new agreement updated provisions on digital trade, intellectual property, labor standards, and environmental protections. Rules of origin for automobiles were tightened, requiring higher percentages of North American content and production by workers earning higher wages. These changes reflected concerns about NAFTA's impacts while maintaining the fundamental free trade framework.

SUPERVISORY IMPLICATIONS

Trade agreements create opportunities and challenges for businesses. Reduced tariffs lower costs for companies importing materials, components, or finished goods. Companies can access larger markets by exporting to partner countries without facing high tariff barriers. This allows businesses to grow beyond domestic markets and diversify revenue sources.

Trade agreements affect competitive dynamics. Domestic companies face increased competition from foreign firms entering their markets with reduced tariffs. Companies must improve efficiency, quality, or innovation to compete effectively. Some businesses benefit from expanded markets while others struggle with increased competition.

Supervisors must understand rules of origin, which determine whether products qualify for preferential tariff treatment under trade agreements. Products must contain specified percentages of content from member countries to receive benefits. Companies maintain documentation proving compliance with these rules to access preferential tariffs.

Trade agreements create supply chain opportunities. Companies can source materials globally, selecting suppliers based on quality, cost, and capabilities rather than being limited by tariff considerations. However, this creates complexity in managing international suppliers, ensuring quality, and coordinating logistics.

Political changes affect trade agreements. The renegotiation of NAFTA into USMCA demonstrated that trade agreements can be modified or terminated based on political pressures and changing priorities. Supervisors should monitor trade policy developments that might affect their businesses.

Understanding trade agreements helps businesses make strategic decisions about market entry, facility location, and supply chain design. Companies can structure operations to optimize benefits from trade agreements while managing risks associated with international commerce.

Sample Test Questions

1) Which of the following is the Title that protects race?

   A) Title IV
   B) Title V
   C) Title VI
   D) Title VII

The correct answer is D:) Title VII.

2) Management by Walking Around (MBWA) is primarily intended to:

   A) Micromanage employees and ensure they are working at all times
   B) Provide managers with unfiltered information through direct observation and informal communication
   C) Replace formal performance reviews and structured meetings
   D) Reduce the need for written reports and documentation

The correct answer is B:) Provide managers with unfiltered information through direct observation and informal communication. MBWA emphasizes personal contact and direct observation to help managers gain accurate understanding of operations, identify problems early, and maintain employee engagement. It complements rather than replaces formal management tools.

3) Which of the following is a potential pitfall of poorly executed Management by Walking Around?

    A) Employees may become too comfortable with management presence
    B) Managers may gather too much accurate information about operations
    C) Employees may interpret frequent visits as intrusive surveillance rather than genuine interest
    D) Production efficiency always decreases when managers are present

The correct answer is C:) Employees may interpret frequent visits as intrusive surveillance rather than genuine interest. Excessive or poorly executed walkarounds can feel threatening to employees who view management presence as monitoring rather than engagement. Managers must balance visibility with giving employees space to work independently.

4) An embargo differs from a tariff in that:

    A) An embargo imposes taxes on imports while a tariff prohibits trade entirely
    B) An embargo typically bars trade entirely while a tariff imposes taxes on imports
    C) Embargoes are always temporary while tariffs are permanent
    D) Embargoes only affect exports while tariffs only affect imports

The correct answer is B:) An embargo typically bars trade entirely while a tariff imposes taxes on imports. Embargoes represent complete prohibitions on trade with specific countries or on particular goods, making such trade illegal. Tariffs allow trade to continue but impose taxes, making imports more expensive.

5) The Office of Foreign Assets Control (OFAC) maintains a list of Specially Designated Nationals (SDNs) to:

    A) Identify individuals and entities with whom U.S. persons are prohibited from doing business
    B) Track all foreign nationals entering the United States
    C) List countries eligible for preferential trade agreements
    D) Document companies that have successfully complied with embargo regulations

The correct answer is A:) Identify individuals and entities with whom U.S. persons are prohibited from doing business. The SDN list helps U.S. companies comply with embargo and sanctions requirements by identifying blocked parties. Companies must screen business partners against this list to avoid violations.

6) Which of the following is part of the macroenvironment rather than the microenvironment?

   A) A company's direct competitors
   B) The company's suppliers
   C) Technological innovations affecting entire industries
   D) The company's immediate customers

The correct answer is C:) Technological innovations affecting entire industries. The macroenvironment consists of broad external forces beyond individual organizational control, including technological, economic, legal, and political factors. The microenvironment includes immediate stakeholders like competitors, suppliers, and customers.

7) The legalization of recreational marijuana in various states primarily represents a change in which macroenvironmental factor?

   A) Technological environment
   B) Legal and political environment
   C) Economic environment
   D) Global environment

The correct answer is B:) Legal and political environment. Changes in laws and regulations governing business operations fall within the legal environment. This example also reflects political decisions about regulation, creating new industries while raising compliance challenges.

8) Exchange rates primarily impact businesses by:

   A) Determining domestic inflation rates
   B) Affecting the relative cost of exports and imports when currencies strengthen or weaken
   C) Setting interest rates for business loans
   D) Establishing tariff levels between countries

The correct answer is B:) Affecting the relative cost of exports and imports when currencies strengthen or weaken. When the U.S. dollar strengthens, American exports become more expensive for foreign buyers while imports become cheaper. Companies engaged in international trade must manage currency risk through hedging or pricing adjustments.

9) Which of the following best describes how automation and robotics affect the macroenvironment?

   A) They only impact individual companies that choose to adopt them
   B) They represent technological changes that transform entire industries and affect workforce requirements
   C) They have no effect on labor markets or employment patterns
   D) They only affect manufacturing and have no impact on service industries

The correct answer is B:) They represent technological changes that transform entire industries and affect workforce requirements. Automation represents a macroenvironmental technological factor affecting manufacturing, warehousing, and service industries broadly. It increases efficiency while also displacing workers and requiring supervisors to manage workforce transitions.

10) The Occupational Safety and Health Administration (OSHA) has authority to:

   A) Set minimum wage requirements for all industries
   B) Inspect workplaces, investigate accidents, issue citations, and impose penalties for safety violations
   C) Negotiate labor union contracts on behalf of workers
   D) Determine which companies can operate in specific industries

The correct answer is B:) Inspect workplaces, investigate accidents, issue citations, and impose penalties for safety violations. OSHA protects worker safety and health by setting and enforcing workplace safety standards. The agency can conduct inspections triggered by complaints or accidents and classify violations by severity.

11) Which regulatory agency would investigate allegations of insider trading?

   A) Environmental Protection Agency (EPA)
   B) Food and Drug Administration (FDA)
   C) Securities and Exchange Commission (SEC)
   D) Occupational Safety and Health Administration (OSHA)

The correct answer is C:) Securities and Exchange Commission (SEC). The SEC regulates securities markets and enforces laws against securities fraud, insider trading, and market manipulation. Insider trading occurs when individuals trade securities based on material non-public information.

12) The Federal Aviation Administration (FAA) is responsible for:

A) Regulating maritime shipping and port operations
B) Certifying aircraft, pilots, and maintenance organizations while overseeing air traffic control
C) Investigating financial crimes in the aviation industry
D) Setting fuel efficiency standards for automobiles

The correct answer is B:) Certifying aircraft, pilots, and maintenance organizations while overseeing air traffic control. The FAA regulates civil aviation to ensure safe and efficient use of national airspace. This includes aircraft certification, pilot licensing, airline oversight, and airport operations.

13) Under the Sarbanes-Oxley Act, public company executives must:

A) Personally certify the accuracy of financial statements
B) Donate a portion of their salary to charity
C) Serve a minimum of five years in their position
D) Hold advanced degrees in accounting

The correct answer is A:) Personally certify the accuracy of financial statements. Sarbanes-Oxley, enacted after accounting scandals at Enron and WorldCom, increased penalties for securities fraud and established requirements for internal controls. Executive certification creates personal accountability for financial reporting accuracy.

14) The Environmental Protection Agency (EPA) regulates all of the following EXCEPT:

A) Air and water quality
B) Hazardous waste management
C) Workplace safety and employee health
D) Chemical safety and pesticide use

The correct answer is C:) Workplace safety and employee health. Workplace safety falls under OSHA's jurisdiction. The EPA focuses on environmental protection, including air quality, water quality, hazardous waste, chemical safety, and pollution control affecting human health and the environment.

15) Gross Domestic Product (GDP) measures:

A) Only goods produced within a country, excluding services
B) The total monetary value of all finished goods and services produced within a country's borders during a specific period
C) Personal income levels of a country's citizens
D) International trade balances between countries

The correct answer is B:) The total monetary value of all finished goods and services produced within a country's borders during a specific period. GDP serves as the primary indicator of economic size and health, typically calculated quarterly and annually. It includes both goods and services.

16) Which of the following is NOT one of the four main components of GDP using the expenditure approach?

A) Consumption
B) Investment
C) Inflation
D) Government spending

The correct answer is C:) Inflation. The four components of GDP using the expenditure approach are consumption (household spending), investment (business capital spending and residential construction), government spending, and net exports (exports minus imports). Inflation is measured separately and used to calculate real GDP from nominal GDP.

17) Real GDP differs from nominal GDP in that real GDP:

A) Only includes services while nominal GDP includes goods
B) Adjusts for inflation using constant prices to allow meaningful comparisons across time
C) Excludes government spending while nominal GDP includes it
D) Only measures international trade while nominal GDP measures domestic production

The correct answer is B:) Adjusts for inflation using constant prices to allow meaningful comparisons across time. Real GDP uses constant prices from a base year, isolating changes in production quantity from price changes. Nominal GDP uses current prices and can increase simply due to inflation without actual production increases.

18) A major limitation of GDP as a measure of economic welfare is that it:

   A) Is too difficult to calculate accurately
   B) Only measures economic activity in developed countries
   C) Excludes non-market activities and doesn't measure income distribution or quality of life
   D) Cannot be compared between different time periods

The correct answer is C:) Excludes non-market activities and doesn't measure income distribution or quality of life. GDP doesn't capture household production, volunteer work, environmental quality, income inequality, or overall happiness. A country could have rising GDP while most citizens experience declining living standards if growth concentrates among the wealthy.

19) The General Agreement on Tariffs and Trade (GATT) was primarily designed to:

   A) Establish a single global currency for international trade
   B) Reduce tariffs and other trade barriers through multilateral negotiations
   C) Create regional trade blocs that excluded non-member countries
   D) Increase tariffs to protect domestic industries from foreign competition

The correct answer is B:) Reduce tariffs and other trade barriers through multilateral negotiations. GATT, established in 1947, provided the foundation for the post-World War II international trading system. Member countries participated in successive negotiation rounds achieving tariff reductions and addressing broader trade issues.

20) The most-favored-nation (MFN) principle under GATT required that:

   A) Developing countries receive preferential treatment over developed nations
   B) Countries extend to all GATT members the best trade terms they offered any single member
   C) Each country could select one "most favored" trading partner for exclusive benefits
   D) Larger economies automatically received better trade terms than smaller ones

The correct answer is B:) Countries extend to all GATT members the best trade terms they offered any single member. This prevented discriminatory trade practices and promoted multilateral trade liberalization. If a country reduced tariffs for one member, it had to offer the same reduction to all GATT members.

21) NAFTA (North American Free Trade Agreement) created a free trade zone between:

   A) The United States, Canada, and Mexico
   B) All countries in North and South America
   C) The United States, Canada, and China
   D) The United States, Mexico, and Brazil

The correct answer is A:) The United States, Canada, and Mexico. NAFTA, implemented in 1994, eliminated most tariffs and trade barriers between these three countries, creating one of the world's largest trading blocs. It was replaced in 2020 by the United States-Mexico-Canada Agreement (USMCA).

22) Which of the following investigates businesses and individuals for enforcement of laws regarding protected classes?

   A) OSHA
   B) EEO
   C) Department of Labor
   D) COBRA

The correct answer is B:) EEO.

23) Which of the following ensures that employees retain access to medical coverage after involuntary termination?

   A) OSHA
   B) EEO
   C) Department of Labor
   D) COBRA

The correct answer is D:) COBRA.

24) Which of the following is NOT a protected Title VII class?

   A) Race
   B) Age
   C) Sexual preference
   D) Religion

The correct answer is C:) Sexual preference.

Principles of Supervision

25) Which of the following is NOT an example of traditional authority?

   A) Supervisor
   B) Vice President
   C) Bishop
   D) Secretary

The correct answer is D:) Secretary.

26) Which of the following is responsible for ensuring employee safety?

   A) OSHA
   B) EEO
   C) Department of Labor
   D) COBRA

The correct answer is A:) OSHA.

27) Which of the following is NOT a way to deal with risk?

   A) Assuming
   B) Avoiding
   C) Shifting
   D) Deflecting

The correct answer is D:) Deflecting.

28) Which of the following is an example of environmental stress?

   A) Construction noise
   B) Strong perfume
   C) Peers
   D) Broken heating unit

The correct answer is A:) Construction noise.

29) Which of the following is an example of Maslow's first level of needs?

   A) Food
   B) Car
   C) School
   D) Church

The correct answer is A:) Food.

30) Which is the second stage of Maslow's Hierarchy of Needs?

   A) Self-actualization
   B) Esteem needs
   C) Safety needs
   D) Physical needs

The correct answer is C:) Safety needs.

31) When you choose the best action for each situation

   A) Situational leadership
   B) Participative leadership
   C) Autocratic leadership
   D) Laissez faire leadership

The correct answer is A:) Situational leadership.

32) When a supervisor asks for opinions in making decisions

   A) Situational leadership
   B) Participative leadership
   C) Autocratic leadership
   D) Laissez faire leadership

The correct answer is B:) Participative leadership.

33) Which of the following is a union function?

   A) Negotiate pay
   B) Creating new business policies
   C) Budgeting
   D) Creating statistical reports

The correct answer is A:) Negotiate pay.

34) Which of the following is an example of Maslow's third level of needs?

   A) Sex
   B) Money
   C) Love
   D) Home

The correct answer is C:) Love.

35) Which of the following is NOT part of a training program?

   A) Job sharing
   B) Job rotating
   C) Temporary promotion
   D) Promotion

The correct answer is D:) Promotion.

36) Which of the following is an industry commonly known to have line employees?

   A) Automotive
   B) Woodworking
   C) Education
   D) Retail

The correct answer is A:) Automotive.

37) Hands off leadership

   A) Situational leadership
   B) Participative leadership
   C) Autocratic leadership
   D) Laissez faire leadership

The correct answer is D:) Laissez faire leadership.

Principles of Supervision

38) Which of the following tells employees and others what is the main purpose of the company is

   A) Vision
   B) Mission statement
   C) Company statement
   D) Business plan

The correct answer is B:) Mission statement.

39) A policy can be defined as a _____ action course that serves as a guide for the identified and accepted objectives and goals.

   A) Predefined
   B) Flexible
   C) Necessary
   D) Unknown

The correct answer is A:) Predefined.

40) A totalitarian leader

   A) Situational leadership
   B) Participative leadership
   C) Autocratic leadership
   D) Laissez faire leadership

The correct answer is C:) Autocratic leadership.

41) Which of the following is NOT a supervisory function?

   A) Marketing
   B) Planning
   C) Staffing
   D) Organizing

The correct answer is A:) Marketing.

42) Which of the following is an example of an extrinsic reward?

   A) Raise
   B) Self-esteem
   C) Praise
   D) Personal development

The correct answer is A:) Raise.

43) If a plant manager is tasked to reduce costs by 10% this is an example of what kind of goal?

   A) Strategic
   B) Long-term
   C) Tactical
   D) Operational

The correct answer is D:) Operational.

44) Which of the following shows the relationship between employees and their peers?

   A) Organizational chart
   B) Gantt chart
   C) Decision tree
   D) Simulation

The correct answer is A:) Organizational chart.

45) Which of the following shows alternate paths for decision making?

   A) Organizational chart
   B) Gantt chart
   C) Decision tree
   D) Simulation

The correct answer is C:) Decision tree.

46) When a supervisor administers a questionnaire among participants that have never met it is called

   A) Brainstorming
   B) Sampling
   C) Delphi technique
   D) Groupthink

The correct answer is C:) Delphi technique.

47) Which of the following shows timelines for projects?

   A) Organizational chart
   B) Gantt chart
   C) Decision tree
   D) Simulation

The correct answer is B:) Gantt chart.

48) Who created Theory X and Theory Y?

   A) Max Weber
   B) Abraham Maslow
   C) Douglas McGregor
   D) Frank Gilbreth

The correct answer is C:) Douglas McGregor.

49) When two groups or individuals work together to resolve a problem it is called

   A) Negotiation
   B) Grievance
   C) Arbitration
   D) Mediation

The correct answer is A:) Negotiation.

50) What is it called when a third party is facilitating negotiations?

   A) Concession
   B) Grievance
   C) Arbitration
   D) Mediation

The correct answer is D:) Mediation.

51) An employee that works on an assembly line performing the same task again and again is an example of

   A) Job specialization
   B) Job rotation
   C) Job sharing
   D) None of the above

The correct answer is A:) Job specialization.

52) Two receptionists work at Widget, Inc., one in the morning and one in the afternoon. They are an example of

   A) Job specialization
   B) Job rotation
   C) Job sharing
   D) None of the above

The correct answer is C:) Job sharing.

53) When a person acts as expected as part of the group they are portraying their

   A) Role
   B) Groupthink
   C) Norm
   D) Status rank

The correct answer is A:) Role.

54) Who first studied job motions with bricklayers, studying how fewer hand motions made the work faster?

A) Max Weber
B) Abraham Maslow
C) Douglas McGregor
D) Frank Gilbreth

The correct answer is D:) Frank Gilbreth.

55) When someone is producing at standard it is called

A) Role
B) Role conflict
C) Norm
D) Status

The correct answer is C:) Norm.

56) What is it called when a third party of empowered to resolve a disagreement it is called?

A) Negotiation
B) Grievance
C) Arbitration
D) Mediation

The correct answer is C:) Arbitration.

57) Who was a proponent of bureaucracy?

A) Max Weber
B) Abraham Maslow
C) Douglas McGregor
D) Frank Gilbreth

The correct answer is A:) Max Weber.

58) What is a formal complaint called?

   A) Negotiation
   B) Grievance
   C) Arbitration
   D) Mediation

The correct answer is B:) Grievance.

59) Which of the following industries is part of a dynamic environment, meaning the market is constantly changing and updating?

   A) Nurseries
   B) Education
   C) Electronics
   D) Manufacturing

The correct answer is C:) Electronics.

60) Which of the following can NOT be discussed in a job interview?

   A) Education and degrees
   B) Children
   C) Previous wages
   D) Personality

The correct answer is B:) Children.

61) To motivate line employees and keep them interested in their work, supervisors may institute any of the following BUT

   A) Job specialization
   B) Job rotation
   C) Mentoring
   D) Four day work weeks

The correct answer is A:) Job specialization.

62) The grapevine of the organization is everything BUT

   A) Formal
   B) Generally accurate
   C) Verbal
   D) Exists in every organization

The correct answer is A:) Formal.

63) When a supervisor believes that all employees like work it is called

   A) Theory Y
   B) Theory X
   C) Hawthorne Effect
   D) TQM

The correct answer is A:) Theory Y.

64) This scientific study originally tested worker's output and light, later revealing unintended consequences

   A) Theory Y
   B) Theory X
   C) Hawthorne Effect
   D) TQM

The correct answer is C:) Hawthorne Effect.

65) Referent power is the same as

   A) Laissez faire leadership
   B) Charismatic leadership
   C) Peer pressure
   D) Expert leadership

The correct answer is B:) Charismatic leadership.

66) Legitimate power is the same as

   A) Laissez faire leadership
   B) Traditional leadership
   C) Peer pressure
   D) Expert leadership

The correct answer is B:) Traditional leadership.

67) Regarding sexual harassment which of the following is NOT true

   A) Offenders can be same or opposite sex
   B) Victims do not have to be harassed personally but affected through environment
   C) Harasser must be a superior employee
   D) Harassment may occur without economic injury

The correct answer is C:) Harasser must be a superior employee.

68) Who created a system of human needs and motivations?

   A) Max Weber
   B) Abraham Maslow
   C) Douglas McGregor
   D) Frank Gilbreth

The correct answer is B:) Abraham Maslow.

69) Long term success through customer satisfaction

   A) Theory Y
   B) Theory X
   C) Hawthorne Effect
   D) TQM

The correct answer is D:) TQM.

70) Who was responsible for developing the 14 principles of management?

    A) Max Weber
    B) Henri Fayol
    C) Douglas McGregor
    D) Frank Gilbreth

The correct answer is B:) Henri Fayol.

71) The way that people communicate with each other using their bodies

    A) Consideration
    B) Body language
    C) Communication
    D) Charisma

The correct answer is B:) Body language.

72) Leadership characteristics that inspire employees is called

    A) Chain of command
    B) Vision
    C) Charisma
    D) Motivation

The correct answer is C:) Charisma.

73) Agreement of members of a group on a decision is called

    A) Consensus
    B) Group think
    C) Meetings
    D) Consideration

The correct answer is A:) Consensus.

74) Leaders that use group ideas to make decisions

    A) Autocratic
    B) Laissez-faire
    C) Democratic
    D) Trait

The correct answer is C:) Democratic.

75) Which is NOT a factor that influences the favorableness of a leader?

A) Leader-member relations
B) Task structure
C) Leader position power
D) Charisma level

The correct answer is D:) Charisma level.

76) Which of the following best describes rule utilitarianism?

A) A person considers an action independently of a situation and determines whether it is more often moral or immoral to determine how to classify it in all situations.
B) A person considers a situation and decides upon the easiest course of action.
C) A person considers an action and determines whether it would end favorably for them.
D) A person examines a situation, considers all possible actions they could take and decides which one would end most favorably for all involved.

The correct answer is A:) A person considers an action independently of a situation and determines whether it is more often moral or immoral to determine how to classify it in all situations.

77) A person is given the opportunity to volunteer at a local food bank. They consider the other things they could do at that time, such as cleaning and watching TV. They know that the work that they do could really benefit people at the food bank, whereas the other activities only benefit themselves. They decide that the service is the best decision for them. What type of ethical theory does their thought process and decision follow?

A) Rule utilitarianism
B) Act utilitarianism
C) Deontological theory
D) Ethical egoism

The correct answer is B:) Act utilitarianism. A person examines a situation, considers all possible actions they could take and decides which one would end most favorably for all involved.

78) Which of the following is NOT a communication pattern?

    A) Chain
    B) Circle
    C) Wheel
    D) Arc

The correct answer is D:) Arc.

79) When someone receives too much information and cannot tell what is important from what is not it is called

    A) Overload
    B) Spam
    C) Decoding information
    D) Rejected information

The correct answer is A:) Overload.

80) When someone deliberately tampers with a message, leaving out information, it is called

    A) Overload
    B) Omitting
    C) Y pattern
    D) Highlighting

The correct answer is B:) Omitting.

81) Which of the following is NOT an organizational theory?

    A) Classical organization
    B) Mechanistic
    C) System
    D) Assembly

The correct answer is D:) Assembly.

82) When information is communicated informally in an organization it is called the

   A) Grapevine
   B) Telephone
   C) Circle
   D) Hub

The correct answer is A:) Grapevine.

83) The organizational structure where a group performing a specialized task reports to a manager in that same area

   A) Functional
   B) Line and staff
   C) Product
   D) Matrix

The correct answer is A:) Functional.

84) The organizational structure where there are staff departments that support other departments

   A) Functional
   B) Line and staff
   C) Product
   D) Matrix

The correct answer is B:) Line and staff.

85) The organizational structure where organizations are structured around a special project or event

   A) Functional
   B) Line and staff
   C) Product
   D) Matrix

The correct answer is D:) Matrix.

86) When you are a secretary and there are seven levels between your role and the CEO, your organization is considered to be

   A) Fat
   B) Tall
   C) Flat
   D) Short

The correct answer is B:) Tall.

87) When the controls of an organization are centralized, the communication between departments will be

   A) Vertical
   B) Horizontal
   C) Directional
   D) Hub and spoke

The correct answer is A:) Vertical.

88) Which of the following is NOT an aspect of an organic organization?

   A) Decentralized control
   B) Horizontal lines of communication
   C) Loose roles
   D) Incentive programs

The correct answer is D:) Incentive programs.

89) When a manager makes a decision then looks for information to justify the decision, it is called

   A) Implicit favorite model
   B) Bounded rationality model
   C) Econological model
   D) None of the above

The correct answer is A:) Implicit favorite model.

90) When you are selecting a new location for a second office, this decision would be considered

   A) Hard
   B) Programmed
   C) Nonprogrammed
   D) Geocentric

The correct answer is C:) Nonprogrammed.

91) When you make a routine, everyday decision it is called

   A) Habit
   B) Programmed
   C) Nonprogrammed
   D) Geocentric

The correct answer is B:) Programmed.

92) When you find the answer to your problem but settle for something else is an example of the

   A) Implicit favorite model
   B) Bounded rationality model
   C) Econological model
   D) None of the above

The correct answer is B:) Bounded rationality model.

93) When you choose the solution that has the greatest benefit for you

   A) Implicit favorite model
   B) Bounded rationality model
   C) Econological model
   D) None of the above

The correct answer is C:) Econological model.

94) Which of the following moral theories considers the action resulting in the greatest benefit to all people as the most moral action?

   A) Act utilitarianism
   B) Rule utilitarianism
   C) Relativism
   D) Deontology

The correct answer is A:) Act utilitarianism. This practice is called maximizing utility.

95) Cost benefit considerations would be most typical of which of type of ethics?

   A) Consequentialism
   B) Egoism
   C) Kantian
   D) Utilitarianism

The correct answer is D:) Utilitarianism. The idea behind utilitarianism is to "maximize utility." In other words the focus is on considering the benefits and costs and if the benefits are greater than the costs then the action is moral.

96) If you are an authoritarian, you ascribe to

   A) Theory X
   B) Theory Y
   C) Theory XY
   D) Management theory

The correct answer is A:) Theory X.

97) The organizational structure where organizations are divided by products or divisions

   A) Functional
   B) Line and staff
   C) Product
   D) Matrix

The correct answer is C:) Product.

98) A manager who believes that all people are valuable and want to contribute to their best ability you ascribe to

   A) Theory X
   B) Theory Y
   C) Theory XY
   D) Management theory

The correct answer is B:) Theory Y.

99) Who believed that managers make decisions based on their assumptions of human nature?

   A) McGregor
   B) Taylor
   C) Ratter
   D) Johnson

The correct answer is A:) McGregor.

100) Which of the following is NOT a contributor to an employee's attitude?

   A) Previous jobs
   B) Education
   C) Peers
   D) Family

The correct answer is B:) Education.

101) When an interest in the people's problems affects the outcome, not the changes themselves, it is known as

   A) Hawthorne Effect
   B) Taylor Effect
   C) Laissez faire Effect
   D) Groupthink Effect

The correct answer is A:) Hawthorne Effect.

102) When a person acts as expected as part of the a group they are portraying their

   A) Role
   B) Groupthink
   C) Norm
   D) Status rank

The correct answer is A:) Role.

103) When someone is producing at standard it is called

   A) Role
   B) Role conflict
   C) Norm
   D) Status

The correct answer is C:) Norm.

104) When an employee puts in extra time and effort with the hopes of receiving a large bonus, this employee is being motivated by

   A) Expectancy
   B) Goal setting
   C) Rewards
   D) Benefits

The correct answer is A:) Expectancy.

105) When your manager completes a job review with you regarding your performance they give you

   A) Feedback
   B) Goals
   C) Equity
   D) Growth

The correct answer is A:) Feedback.

106) Which is the final stage of Maslow's Hierarchy of Needs?

   A) Self-actualization
   B) Esteem needs
   C) Belonging and love
   D) Safety

The correct answer is A:) Self-actualization.

107) Which defense mechanism occurs when someone transfers their thoughts and feelings onto others?

   A) Denial
   B) Suppression
   C) Reaction formation
   D) Projection

The correct answer is D:) Projection.

108) Which is the first stage of Maslow's Hierarchy of Needs?

   A) Self-actualization
   B) Esteem needs
   C) Safety
   D) Physical needs

The correct answer is D:) Physical needs.

109) When communication is given from the CEO to his subordinates it is called

   A) Top down
   B) Bottom up
   C) Hub
   D) Spoke

The correct answer is A:) Top down.

110) The intent of the Sarbanes-Oxley Act was to

A) Help companies be better able to deal with the ethical problems raised by increased technology.
B) Restore stakeholder confidence in the securities market after a series of scandals in the early 2000s.
C) Create a commission that would monitor the accounting records of major businesses.
D) Scare businesses into conforming with the GAAP standards in their accounting practices.

The correct answer is B:) Restore stakeholder confidence in the securities market after a series of scandals in the early 2000s.

111) Information that is difficult to measure is called

A) Quantitative
B) Qualitative
C) Longitudinal
D) Dependent

The correct answer is B:) Qualitative.

112) If you believe that all people are good – you ascribe to this school of thought

A) Biological
B) Cognitive
C) Structuralism
D) Humanistic

The correct answer is D:) Humanistic.

113) Standards or principles

A) Norms
B) Values
C) Rules
D) Status quo

The correct answer is B:) Values.

114) Which of the following is NOT a factor with job satisfaction?

   A) Hours
   B) Pay
   C) Benefits
   D) Vacation location

The correct answer is D:) Vacation location.

115) When a person responds to a neutral stimulus _____ is being used.

   A) Classical conditioning
   B) Operant conditioning
   C) Extrinsic reinforcer
   D) Intrinsic reinforcer

The correct answer is A:) Classical conditioning.

116) Getting a scholarship because of good grades is an example of

   A) Extrinsic reinforcement
   B) Intrinsic reinforcement
   C) Motivation
   D) ERG theory

The correct answer is A:) Extrinsic reinforcement.

117) Risks to the organization when individuals have chronic stress include all BUT the following

   A) High turnover
   B) Aggression in the workplace
   C) Absenteeism
   D) High morale

The correct answer is D:) High morale.

118) Which of the following is the second step when forming a group?

    A) Storming
    B) Norming
    C) Forming
    D) Conforming

The correct answer is A:) Storming.

119) How well the group works together is called

    A) Dynamics
    B) Cohesiveness
    C) Conforming
    D) Norming

The correct answer is B:) Cohesiveness.

120) Which of the following is NOT a contingency theory of leadership?

    A) Path-goal model
    B) Life cycle model
    C) Vroom-Yetton model
    D) ERG theory

The correct answer is D:) ERG theory. The ERG is a theory of motivation, not leadership.

121) Leaders that centralize power and decisions in themselves

    A) Autocratic
    B) Laissez-faire
    C) Democratic
    D) Trait

The correct answer is A:) Autocratic.

122) Statistics belong to which "family"?

   A) Supervision
   B) Management
   C) Science
   D) Auditing

The correct answer is C:) Science.

123) Six Sigma strives for

   A) Perfect attendance
   B) Improvements in ethnic quotas
   C) Less environmental impact
   D) Perfection in processes and product

The correct answer is D:) Perfection in processes and product. For a company to be a perfect Six Sigma, they must have no more than 3.4 defects per million opportunities.

124) Which contingency theory focuses on the readiness of the employees?

   A) Path-goal model
   B) Life cycle model
   C) Vroom-Yetton model
   D) Fiedler model

The correct answer is B:) Life cycle model.

125) Which of the following companies was NOT implicated in a scandal in the early 2000s?

   A) Enron
   B) Coca-Cola
   C) Tyco International
   D) All of the above were implicated in scandals

The correct answer is D:) All of the above were implicated in scandals. Due to the various different scandals occurring in the early 2000s, federal regulations concerning businesses were tightened. One example of this is the Sarbanes-Oxley Act.

126) Who was the author of the path-goal theory?

   A) Victor Vroom
   B) Robert House
   C) Arthur Jago
   D) Philip Yetton

The correct answer is B:) Robert House.

127) Which of the following are barriers to making decisions?

   A) Statistics
   B) Lack of statistics
   C) Emotions
   D) All of the above

The correct answer is D:) All of the above.

128) Which of the following is NOT a level of management according to Henri Fayol?

   A) Planning
   B) Organization
   C) Commanding
   D) All of the above are levels of management

The correct answer is D:) All of the above are levels of management. Henri Fayol's identified six levels of management functions. These levels are forecasting, planning, organization, commanding, coordinating and controlling.

129) Which of the following moral theories is NOT consequentialist?

   A) Teleology
   B) Act utilitarianism
   C) Egoism
   D) Kantian ethics

The correct answer is D:) Kantian ethics. Kantian ethics determines morality based on the morality of the action itself, not its consequences. It is deontological.

130) Utilitarianism is a type of

   A) Consequentialism
   B) Relativism
   C) Deontological ethics
   D) Egoism

The correct answer is A:) Consequentialism. Utilitarianism considers the consequences of an action and the extent to which they benefit society in determining morality, therefore it is consequential.

131) Fast food places do not pay their workers less than minimum wage because it is against the law. Which of Kohlberg's stages does this describe?

   A) Stage 1
   B) Stage 2
   C) Stage 3
   D) Stage 4

The correct answer is D:) Stage 4. In Stage 4, people are motivated primarily by authority, such as the law.

132) A billboard is an example of

   A) Active listening
   B) Two-way communication
   C) One-way communication
   D) None of the above

The correct answer is C:) One-way communication.

133) Leaders that give the group total freedom

   A) Autocratic
   B) Laissez-faire
   C) Democratic
   D) Trait

The correct answer is B:) Laissez-faire.

134) A worker who is always honest with their cash drawer must be a good mother as well because she is "honest" and "honest" people raise good children. This thought process describes

   A) Discrimination
   B) Trait management
   C) The halo effect
   D) Laissez-faire

The correct answer is C:) The halo effect. The halo effect is when one person's positive or negative traits influence their other traits.

135) The parity principle stems from

   A) A manager delegating a task
   B) Union pay negotiations
   C) One-way communication
   D) None of the above

The correct answer is A:) A manager delegating a task. The manager should give the employee the resources and independence to complete the task the manager has given him. The employee should use those resources needed, but no more than necessary.

136) Which of the following statements is FALSE?

   A) Type B personalities are generally less efficient than Type A personalities because they are so relaxed.
   B) Type A personalities and type B personalities are both efficient, they just do things different ways.
   C) Type B personalities are laid back and casual, which makes them unhealthy and increases their risks.
   D) Type A personalities are generally less efficient than Type B personalities because they have so many focuses that they never get any one project finished.

The correct answer is B:) Type A personalities and type B personalities are both efficient, they just do things different ways.

137) The hot stove method of discipline includes which of the following?

   A) A warning
   B) Immediate discipline/consequence
   C) Consistent application
   D) All of the above

The correct answer is D:) All of the above.

138) Herzberg believed that increasing which of the following would increase job satisfaction?

   A) Breadth
   B) Job enlargement
   C) Hygiene
   D) Depth

The correct answer is D:) Depth. Depth is related to job enrichment, which was Herzberg's focus.

139) Some people believe that women earn less than men because female held jobs have been historically devalued, and that women should be given equal pay for equal work. This belief is called

   A) Comparable worth
   B) Affirmative action
   C) Glass ceiling
   D) Absenteeism

The correct answer is A:) Comparable worth. The idea is that jobs typically held by women receive lower pay on average than jobs typically held by men. Advocates of comparable worth work to ensure that jobs typically held by women that require the same amount of effort and risk as jobs typically held by men (even though they may not be similar) receive equal pay.

140) Which of the following is NOT true of sexual harassment?

   A) The claimant must be able to prove a hostile work environment was created.
   B) Sexual harassment is any repeated, unwanted behavior of a sexual nature.
   C) Sexual harassment can apply to physical actions, words, images and written material.
   D) The primary factor in sexual harassment cases is the intent of the action.

The correct answer is D:) The primary factor in sexual harassment cases is the intent of the action. On the contrary, the primary factor is the effect of the action, or how it is perceived, not the intent.

141) Which of the following is NOT a type of discrimination investigated by the EEOC?

   A) Gender
   B) Disability
   C) Education
   D) Religion

The correct answer is C:) Education. The EEOC investigates situations of discrimination based on age, gender, disability, race, color or religion.

142) The EEOC investigates violations of the

   A) WARN Act
   B) Kyoto Protocol
   C) Sarbanes-Oxley Act
   D) Civil Rights Act of 1964

The correct answer is D:) Civil Rights Act of 1964.

143) Which person created the five management functions?

   A) Frank Gilbreth
   B) Peter Drucker
   C) Henri Fayol
   D) Max Weber

The correct answer is C:) Henri Fayol. Henri Fayol is credited with creating the five management functions which are (1) planning, (2) organizing, (3) commanding, (4) coordinating, and (5) controlling.

144) Which of the following is NOT a type of resistance?

   A) Logical
   B) Psychological
   C) Sociological
   D) Biological

The correct answer is D:) Biological.

145) Which are friendships which cause the development of in-groups and out-groups?

   A) Unions
   B) Fraternities
   C) Vertical-dyad linkages
   D) Group contributions

The correct answer is C:) Vertical-dyad linkages. These are friendships which cause the development of in-groups and out-groups in a working environment. The in-groups receive favorable treatment such as interesting assignments, promotions and raises. The out-groups are the groups which do not share the mutual respect and obligations of a vertical-dyad linkage, and therefore are at a disadvantage. In-group workers tend to be more productive and enthusiastic.

146) Which of the following is NOT a part of the path-goal theory?

   A) Provides a clear path
   B) Helps remove barriers to the problems
   C) Increases the rewards along and at the end of the route
   D) None of the above

The correct answer is D:) None of the above. All of the above answer choices are a part of the path-goal theory.

147) Factor that always stays the same

   A) Dependent variable
   B) Independent variable
   C) Constant
   D) Correlation

The correct answer is C:) Constant.

148) When a person is responsible for the outcome of completing a task well it is called

   A) Sociological
   B) ERG Theory
   C) Indefensible
   D) Accountable

The correct answer is D:) Accountable.

149) Which of the following was established first?

   A) GATT
   B) NAFTA
   C) WTO
   D) A and B were established at the same time

The correct answer is A:) GATT. GATT (General Agreement on Trade and Tariffs) and NAFTA (North American Free Trade Agreement) are the two primary international trade agreements in the United States. GATT was established in 1948 and NAFTA was established in 1994.

150) Which of the following is NOT a consumer protection right?

   A) Right to return products without restriction (Right of Return Act)
   B) Protection against misleading advertisements (Truth in Advertising Laws)
   C) Fair and clear lending practices (Truth in Lending Act)
   D) Purchased items will work properly (warranty protections)

The correct answer is A:) Right to return products without restriction (Right of Return Act). There are many consumer protection laws that protect both consumers and suppliers in the United States. These laws include provisions for price, information, warranties, credit, lending, and other aspects. The right to return a product, however, is based on individual agreements between consumers and suppliers.

151) A ban on trade is known as a(n)

   A) Tariff
   B) Embargo
   C) Restraint
   D) Fare

The correct answer is B:) Embargo. An embargo occurs when a nation bans trade with another nation. Typically it is used as a political maneuver to cause distress to the rival nation's economy. An alternative is high tariffs (or taxes) on imported goods.

152) Which Federal agency would handle claims of workplace discrimination?

   A) North American Employment Equality Agreement
   B) General Agreement on Tariffs and Trade
   C) Equal Employment Opportunities Commission
   D) Fair Employment Practice Commission

The correct answer is C:) Equal Employment Opportunities Commission. The commission was established under the Civil Rights Act in 1964 and it reviews over 100,000 cases per year. The EEOC covers discrimination based on age, ethnicity, gender, disability, and many other matters.

153) What does "T" represent in the SWOT matrix?

   A) Threats
   B) Tariffs
   C) Taxes
   D) Talents

The correct answer is A:) Threats. The SWOT matrix is used to determine the merits of a particular business move. The acronym stands for strengths, weaknesses, opportunities, and threats.

154) Which of the following BEST describes groupthink?

   A) A pattern of group oriented negotiation and reasoning to lead to the most efficient outcome
   B) A program that allows coworkers to brainstorm ideas and discuss projects over the internet
   C) A phenomenon in which individuals desire group harmony and consensus and will not voice dissent
   D) A working style in which desks are arranged in a circular fashion to encourage collaboration

The correct answer is C:) A phenomenon in which individuals desire group harmony and consensus and will not voice dissent. Groupthink can lead to less optimal decision making because employees will wish to follow the group mindset rather than push for change.

155) A start-up company sets goals and standards for themselves based on the performance of their competitors. This is an example of

    A) Groupthink
    B) MBWA
    C) SWOT
    D) Benchmarking

The correct answer is D:) Benchmarking. Benchmarking involves setting goals and measuring progress. It is a common way of monitoring business health, and also incorporating new practices that have been successful for others.

156) Which of the following is NOT characteristic of management by walking around?

    A) Large, secluded management offices
    B) Employees comfortable with approaching management
    C) High levels of contact between management and employees
    D) Increased productivity and morale

The correct answer is A:) Large, secluded management offices. Management by walking around, is a much more open style of management. Managers will spend less time in their own offices and more time with employees. This allows employees to feel more connected with managers and they will be more open to discussing problems and have an increased sense of morale.

157) Which of the following is NOT a need associated with McClelland's Human Motivation Theory?

    A) Achievement
    B) Happiness
    C) Affiliation
    D) Power

The correct answer is B:) Happiness. McClelland's three motivations are achievement, affiliation and power. These needs are learned with time and each individual is motivated by a desire to obtain them.

158) Bureaucratic control emphasizes which organizational element?

   A) Hierarchy and authority
   B) Budget and market influences
   C) Benchmarking statistics
   D) Product quality assurance

The correct answer is A:) Hierarchy and authority. Bureaucratic control is the rules, regulations, and standards that an organization follows in terms of the management hierarchy. Organizations that exhibit strong bureaucratic controls have systems in which the employees do not act without the approval of management.

159) The ability of consumers to influence price or other market aspects is known as

   A) Distribution control
   B) Bureaucratic control
   C) Price control
   D) Market control

The correct answer is D:) Market control. Market control is typically strongly connected with the balance of consumers and providers. More providers and fewer purchasers will result in greater market control. The consumers will have more power to influence the providers and control their actions.

Test Taking Strategies

Here are some test-taking strategies that are specific to this test and to other DSST tests in general:

- Keep your eyes on the time. Pay attention to how much time you have left.
- Read the entire question and read all the answers. Many questions are not as hard to answer as they may seem. Sometimes, a difficult sounding question really only is asking you how to read an accompanying chart. Chart and graph questions are on most DANTES/DSST tests and should be an easy free point.
- If you don't know the answer immediately, the new computer-based testing lets you mark questions and come back to them later if you have time.
- Read the wording carefully. Some words can give you hints to the right answer. There are no exceptions to an answer when there are words in the question such

as always, all or none. If one of the answer choices includes most or some of the right answers, but not all, then that is not the answer. Here is an example:

The primary colors include all of the following:
- A) Red, Yellow, Blue, Green
- B) Red, Green, Yellow
- C) Red, Orange, Yellow
- D) Red, Yellow, Blue

Although item A includes all the right answers, it also includes an incorrect answer, making it incorrect. If you didn't read it carefully, were in a hurry, or didn't know the material well, you might fall for this.

- Make a guess on a question that you do not know the answer to. There is no penalty for an incorrect answer. Eliminate the answer choices that you know are incorrect. For example, this will let your guess be a 1 in 3 chance instead.

Legal Note

All rights reserved. This Study Guide, Book and Flashcards are protected under the US Copyright Law. No part of this book or study guide or flashcards may be reproduced, distributed or stored in a retrieval system, or transmitted in any form or by any means, electronic, mechanical, photocopying, recording, or otherwise, without the prior written permission of the publisher Breely Crush Publishing, LLC.

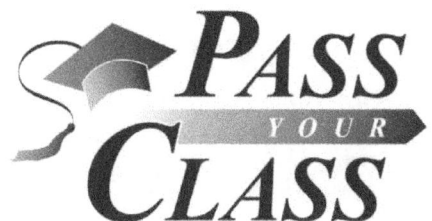

FLASHCARDS

This section contains flashcards for you to use to further your understanding of the material and test yourself on important concepts, names or dates. Read the term or question then flip the page over to check the answer on the back. Keep in mind that this information may not be covered in the text of the study guide. Take your time to study the flashcards, you will need to know and understand these concepts to pass the test.

OSHA

EEO

COBRA

Situational leadership

Participative leadership

Mission statement

Extrinsic reward

Instrinsic reward

Equal Employment Opportunity	Occupational Safety and Health Administration
When you choose the best action for each situation	Comprehensive Omnibus Budget Reconciliation Act
Tells employees and others what is the main purpose of the company is	When a supervisor asks for opinions in making decisions
A reward that comes from within such as self-esteem	A reward that comes externally from a person such as a raise

Organizational Chart	Decision tree
Delphi technique	Gantt chart
Theory X	Theory Y
TQM stands for	TQM's goal is

Shows alternate paths for decision making	Shows the relationship between employees and their peers
Shows timelines for projects	When a supervisor administers a questionnaire among participants that have never met
When a supervisor believes that all employees like work it is called	When a supervisor believes that all employees are lazy and dislike work
Long-term success through customer satisfaction	Total Quality Management

Henri Fayol	Hawthorne Effect
Charisma	Information that is difficult to measure is called
Functional	Line and staff
Matrix	Autocratic leadership

When an interest in people changes the effect on the output	Responsible for developing the 14 principles of management
Qualitative	Leadership characteristics that inspire employees
The organizational structure where there are staff departments support other departments	The organizational structure where a group performing a specialized task reports to a manager in that same area
When the leader keeps the power and makes decisions alone	The organizational structure where organizations are structured around a special project or event

Four stages of groups	**Hierarchy of needs**
Who created Theory X & Theory Y?	**Traditional authority**
Objectives	**Policy**
The core of planning	**Limiting factor**

Maslow's	Forming, Storming, Norming, Conforming
Given to those with a specific title or function such as supervisor or Vice President	Douglas McGregor
A predetermined action course that serves as a guide for the identified and accepted objectives and goals	Goals of an organization towards accomplishment of which all organizational activities are directed
Something which stands in the way of achieving a goal	Decision making

Classical organizational theory	The Mechanistic Theory
What are the two types of organizational structures?	Line employee
In centralization all authority is concentrated where?	In a matrix organization a worker has how many bosses?
Empowerment	Four elements in a control system

Organizational change is inevitable and that organizations and people within the organizations have no other choice except following natural law	Division of labor, vertical and horizontal specialization, etc.
Someone who works on any type of assembly line, manufacturing, etc.	Wide span and narrow span
Two	At the top
Standards, measurement of performance, causal analysis, corrective action	Allowing employees to make their own decisions to help customers

Loading	Forward scheduling
Backward scheduling	Whistle blowing
Terminated	Compensation
Job enrichment	How often should a performance review take place?

Starts today and works out the schedule date for each operation in order to find out the completion date for the order	Working out of hours required to perform each operation
When an employee reports to the media or the government about a company's wrong doings	Starts with the date on which the completed order is needed in the stores department for shipping, then works out backwards to determine the relevant release date for the order
Salary and benefits	Fired
Yearly	Adding more job responsibilities

Business ethics	Studied operant conditioning
Laissez Fare Leadership	Stress
Procedures	Training
Staffing	Just-in-time inventory

B. F. Skinner	A collection of principles and codes of conduct that affect
A person's response to change	A hands-off leadership approach with little supervision
A program built primarily to assist employee development	A plan that shows what methods are to be used
An inventory management system in which inventory arrives only when it is needed	A systematic and methodical filling up of positions

Methods of risk management	**Avoiding the risk**
Operations Research	**Employee counseling**
Systems Theory	**Group dynamics**
Decentralization	**Classification method**

Avoiding certain industries	Assuming the risk, minimizing the risk, avoiding the risk or shifting the risk
Counseling available for employees typically offered through a medical plan	Considers various factors to build a mathematical decision making formula
Deals with role playing coupled with simulation which seek to emphasize group behavior	Deals with interdependence instead of independence of variables
Defines grades for requirements that are found common to various tasks	Decision making is widely dispersed

Ranking system	**Controlling**
Unions	**Personnel records**
Personnel appraisal	**Directing**
Personnel administration	**United States Departement of Labor**

Determining if the methods being used adequately match planned results	Determines salary according to a ranking based on overall importance and responsibilities
Give all the data in the application along with education records, test scores and other factors	Formal associations of employees to represent employees in negotiations with management
Leadership + Motivation + Communication	Helps the employee to know their strengths, weaknesses, opportunities and threats
Makes sure that companies are in compliance with federal employment laws	Looks into manpower resources, aims at harmonious labor, works to achieve organization goals and keeps records

Organizational development	Methods of recruiting
Productivity	Managerial function
Factor comparison	Morale boosting
Shifting the risk	Operative function

Newspaper and television ads, headhunters, staffing firms, word of mouth, etc.	Methodical approach which seeks to improve organizational effectiveness
Planning, organizing, directing and controlling	Output/Input
Makes sure that companies are in compliance with federal employment laws	Points are allotted and wage rates for such key jobs
Recruiting, developing, compensating and keeping records	Purchasing insurance policies

Points system	**Minimizing the risk**
Assuming the risk	**Budgets**
Eustress	**Risk analysis**
Communication	**Motivation**

Screening employees, network passwords, etc.	Requirements appropriate to each job are analyzed and quantified
Statements of targeted results reduced to quantifiable terms	Setting aside enough money to pay for potential losses
Tells you what probabilities are there to arrive at decisional outcomes	Stress that is used positively for personal growth
The more motivated an employee is, the higher their work ability	The main purpose is to influence action and achieve goals

Lead time	Methods of discipline
Collective bargaining	Vertical specialization
Horizontal specialization	Delegation
On-the-job training	Supervisor

Verbal warnings, written warnings, suspension and termination	The time it takes to get an inventory item (from ordering to arrival)
When delegation is done through an existing line of authority	When a group with similar interests bargains as a unit
When supervisors pass on parts of their required tasks to others	When one position is divided among more than one person
Works with people and groups to achieving organization goals	When you learn the job by actually doing it

Affirmative action	ISO
Three first professions	Paternalism
Retributive justice	Destributive justice
Balancing harms	"All the Law and the Prophets hang upon the Two Great Commandments, to love thy Lord God and to love thy neighbor."

International Organization for Standardization	Benefiting underrepresented groups by taking factors such as race, gender, or religion into account in business and educational settings
The way people are governed or treated by an authority	Medicine, law and the ministry
With a strict or radical form of equality that is said to be necessary for all people	Theory that punishments are justified because criminals create an imbalance in the order of society which has to be taken care of by action
Jesus Christ, New Testament	Balancing the harms that exist in both sides of the example of an ethical situation

Paradox	**Prohairesis**
Dihairesis	**Mary Wollstonecraft**
Lawrence Kohlberg	**Environmental racism**
Goal of feminism	**What are stem cells?**

Called the distinguishing factor that separated human beings from all other creatures on the planet	Something that seems to be contradictory and yet my nonetheless be true
Feminist philosopher and writer	The judgement itself that was made by a person's Prohairesis
Any practice which harms an environment that is low income, or where a specific race (often minority) is prevalent, more than it does other environments	Moral development was a sixstage process
Cells which have the potential to beome any type of cell	Complete equality between women and men

www.ingramcontent.com/pod-product-compliance
Lightning Source LLC
Chambersburg PA
CBHW081824300426
44116CB00014B/2481